START YOUR DAY
IN A PRAYERFUL WAY

—— ⌒〜 ——

St. Pantaleon will hear your prayer if you wake up with a headache. He is also the Patron Saint of doctors and can be invoked against loneliness or accidents.

If you are a businesswoman, you may want to start your day by calling upon *St. Margaret Clitherow*.

St. Ferdinand III will come to the aid of parents with large families and farmers in need of rain can pray to *St. Isidore*.

St. Lydwin will give special attention to anyone who wants to skate or rollerblade with safety. If you're going skiing, *St. Bernard of Montjoux* is your Saint, and if you're planning any kind of vacation *St. Anthony of Padua* will guide you.

One of the most popular of all Saints, *St. Agnes of Rome* is the Patron Saint of engaged couples and *St. Dorothy of Caesarea* will hear the prayers of newlyweds.

In good times, and bad, each hour of the day, there is comfort in knowing there is a special Patron Saint to hear your prayer.

EVERYDAY SAINTS

HENRY SCHLESINGER

AVON BOOKS ◆ NEW YORK

EVERYDAY SAINTS is an original publication of Avon Books. This work has never before appeared in book form.

AVON BOOKS
A division of
The Hearst Corporation
1350 Avenue of the Americas
New York, New York 10019

First Avon Books Printing: March 1996

AVON TRADEMARK REG. U.S. PAT. OFF. AND IN OTHER COUNTRIES, MARCA REGIS-TRADA, HECHO EN U.S.A.

Printed in the U.S.A.

RA 10 9 8 7 6 5 4 3 2 1

Dedicated to all in whom the spirits
of Saint Augustine and Saint Aquinas live

CONTENTS

—— ∾ ——————————————

What is it exactly that the Saints bring into our everyday lives? What spiritual nourishment do they offer those involved in the secular world?

Certainly, we turn to them in our times of need, praying for intercession or invoking them against catastrophe. All too often, it is only in our darkest moments that we turn to them for help and inspiration. And often they answer us.

Yet, in our busy lives we tend to think of them not nearly enough. For too many of us, when all is well, they remain far from our daily thoughts. Regrettably, this is not to our credit. For those who seek the help of Saints only in time of need abandon their spiritual search prematurely.

The Saints offer us more than assistance in our times of need. They offer, if we listen, spiritual guidance through their wisdom and example. For even those who left no written record of their own words show us what is possible by the grace and goodness of God's love. Their devotion and love of Jesus allows us to see the always-heroic struggle for perfection of spiritual love.

By their own frequent admissions, they were not perfect. As Saint Clare wrote, they were mere "patterns" and "mirrors" of Christ's true perfection. Wholly human, though touched with divine insight, they struggled against the same temptations we ourselves encounter in our daily lives. It is for this reason that they remain such a strong spiritual force.

They are, to cast them in a modern term, a Christian's true "role models." To speak of so-called role models today means for all too many the more secular personalities and talents of the media or sports field. However much pleasure or entertainment they may provide, their performance on or off the field or camera's eye cannot be called divinely inspired. To look to them as true models of a Christian life is false and self-deceiving. Instead, every day it seems that another one of their number is overtaken by scandal or revealed as venal and depraved. And while we may hold them responsible for their moral weaknesses, was it not a weakness in ourselves that sought some measure of inspiration where none could be expected?

For the young in particular, this is saddening. Because in the repeated revelations of flaws in those they admire, they soon come to learn that failing is inevitable. And, in the worst cases, barely a cause for shame or repentence.

We live in an age, they say, in which we lack heroes. Yet, the Saints' lives were the most heroic in history. They lived and very often died for their faith. They met adversity without complaint and suffered for the greater glory of God.

In our study of the Saints and their lives we are able to see the true possibilities of a Christian life in Jesus Christ. Even the most cursory study of the Saints' lives will show that no barrier was capable of withstanding the strength of faith that would draw them closer to God and Jesus. Born into poverty and into unimaginable opulence, they listened to their hearts, letting their spirits rise to God and in the process, often forsaking worldly possessions as well as sacrificing their lives for their faith.

I am particularly reminded of Mother Katherine Drexel. Born in 1858 to unimaginable wealth, she donated her vast fortune to charity. Dedicating her life to missionary work in opening schools for Native Americans and African-Americans, she worked tirelessly until the age of seventy-seven, when a heart attack required her to curtail her works and devote the remaining nineteen years of her life to prayer and devotions.

Less than forty years following her death, the Wall

Street firm that bore her family name collapsed under the weight of greed and corruption. The architects of the firm's demise suffered jail and humiliation for their unscrupulous acts.

Yet, today, Mother Drexel's good works live on. Through her faith and devotion she touched the lives of millions of people and remains beloved. Yet, the Wall Street firm, which once strangely prided itself on its own avarice and the kingly fortunes it made, has vanished completely.

Today, Saints such as Mother Katherine Drexel speak to us in words and deeds over the vast span of centuries. A thousand years and many continents may divide us from their blessed lives, yet as Christians we are able to understand and marvel at their spiritual achievements. Such is the power of their faith that they are still capable of holding our imaginations in awe and turning our hearts toward the Lord.

Coming to them with a clear eye and an open heart, we may easily see that their deeds and words are as fresh and alive today as when they were first acted or written. Such is the glory of faith. The years cannot tarnish it, just as temptation cannot hold sway over it. Their inspiration, if we allow it to, can turn us once again on the right road.

This book is not intended as a full reference guide to the Saints' lives. Nor is this book intended to provide an in-depth look at the Saints' lives. It is intended for daily reference over a wide range of subjects. Longer books, each devoted to a single Saint, are readily available in libraries and bookstores.

The short histories and quotations contained in these pages are meant to bring their wisdom and lives into a manageable, compact form. No doubt some of the more popular Saints have been omitted and some of the so-called more obscure Saints have been included. Also, for reasons of brevity the full patronage of each Saint has not been included although some are included two or more times.

The intent of this book is to offer a spiritual reminder of the relevance of the Saints' lives in our own lives today. It was written with the intent of offering spiritual comfort to those facing a time of need and to reawaken feelings of awe in those who have perhaps lost sight of the value of Saints in their everyday lives.

Intercession

When we pray to the Saints, we ask for their prayers in Heaven. It is said that just as they loved and cherished their neighbors during their lives on earth, so too, they love and cherish them in Heaven. According to the Scriptures, the intercession of the Saints is among the most important services to God. Just as we may pray for others or ask others to pray for us, so too, the Saints may pray for us. Neither death nor time represents a barrier between the Saints and ourselves.

It should be made clear that Saints do not mediate directly with God. That privilege is Christ's alone. ''I exhort therefore, that first of all, supplications, prayers, intercessions and giving of thanks, be made for all men; for kings, and for all that are in authority; that we may lead a quiet and peaceable life in all godliness and honesty. For this is good and acceptable in the sight of God our Saviour; Who will have all men to be saved, and to come unto the knowledge of truth. For there is one God, and one mediator between God and man, the man Christ Jesus; who gave himself a ransom for all, to be testified in due time.'' (I Timothy 2: 1–5)

Asking for the Saints' intercession through their prayers does not reduce Jesus, but rather joins us all as Christians. Our prayers to the Saints link us most fully not only with the kingdom of Heaven, but with those who accepted God's gift.

O happy saints who rejoice in God; After having passed through the tempestuous sea of this life, you have merited to arrive at the port of eternal repose and sovereign peace where, sheltered from tempests and peril, you are made partakers of endless glory and happiness. I beseech you, by the charity with which your souls are replenished, to regard us with a favorable eye. You are at the brilliant portals of the heavenly Jerusalem; grant us an entrance into that holy city. You are on the mountain of the Lord; draw toward you those who are yet in the valley of tears. Your feet are firmly fixed upon the rock, according to the words of the holy Scripture, since you are confirmed in face and charity; sustain those who still walk in the slippery and perilous path of this life, and who are continually exposed to the fatal falls and mortal wounds of sin. In a word, you are the saints and favorites of God; plead our cause before Him with so much force and ardor, and ask him so earnestly to associate us with you, that we may one day be so happy as to bless eternally His mercies, and testify to you our gratitude forever.

—Saint Augustine

Words of Divine Wisdom

Without work it is impossible to have fun.
—Saint Thomas Aquinas

Seek first the kingdom of heaven and its justice and all things shall be added unto you.
—Matthew

Hell is full of the talented, but Heaven of the energetic.
Jeanne-Françoise de Chantal

The patient and humble endurance of the cross— whatever nature it may be—is the highest work we have to do.
—Katherine Drexel

The chief thing is to take the burden on one's shoulders. As you press forward, it soon shakes down and the load is evenly distributed.
—John Bosco

The honors of this world, what are they but puff and emptiness and peril of falling?
—Saint Augustine

Our Lord has created persons for all states in life, and in all of them we see people who have achieved sanctity by fulfilling their obligations well.
—Saint Anthony Claret

Apothecaries (pharmacists) have almost all kinds of poison for their use, as circumstances may require, but they are not poisoned, because they keep their poi-

sons not in their bodies, but in their shops. In like manner you may possess riches without being poisoned by them, provided you have them for use in your house or in your purse, and not, by love, in your heart.
—SAINT FRANCIS DE SALES

Ambition is the mother of hypocrisy and prefers to skulk in corners and dark places. It cannot endure the light of day. It is an unclean vice wallowing in the depths, always hidden, but with ever an eye to advancement.
—SAINT BERNARD

Men desire authority for its own sake that they may bear a rule, command and control other men, and live uncommanded and uncontrolled themselves.
—SAINT THOMAS MORE

If you have too much to do, with God's help you will find time to do it all.
—SAINT PETER CANISIUS

There are those who clean out stables, cart dung, perform in humble obedience the most abject tasks and are therefore treated as the scum of humanity and earn a crust of bread by the sweat of their brow. But although men despise their life as worthless and contemptible, in the eyes of God it is praiseworthy and of great price.
—JOHN OF MONTMIRAIL

Not to enable the poor to share in our goods is to steal from them and deprive them of life.
—SAINT JOHN CHRYSOSTOM

What men call fame is, after all, but a very windy thing. A man thinks that many are praising him, and talking of him alone, and yet they spend but a very small

*part of the day thinking of him, being occupied with
things of their own.*
—SAINT THOMAS MORE

*Occupations that are necessary and result from God's
ordinance are inevitable, but untimely occupations
should be rejected and preference given to prayer.*
—SAINT MARK THE ASCETIC

*When a man does his work diligently for the sake of
God, it is not a distraction but a thoroughness,
which pleases God.*
—SAINT BARSANUPHIUS

ACCOUNTANTS, BOOKKEEPERS, AND BANKERS

Saint Matthew the Apostle
  First century A.D.

An apostle and evangelist, Matthew was called by Christ from his profession as a tax collector for the Romans at Capernaum. He is the author of the First Gospel. Both Mark and Luke knew him by the name Levi and he may have been known by both names. Very little is known of his following life. There are notes that he was martyred in Persia (Iran) or Ethiopia or some other location, though these remain unsubstantiated.

Saint Matthew is also the Patron Saint of tax collectors, customs officers, money changers, alcoholics, hospitals, fatal diseases, fishermen, and ships.

Feast Day: September 21

Saint Genesius the Comedian
  Died A.D. 300

While performing a parody of a Christian baptism before Emperor Diocletian, he became suddenly converted and declared his faith. So great was his divinely inspired performance, that the emperor, a pagan, became enraged and had Genesius tortured. When the converted actor would not deny his faith, the ruler had him beheaded.

Saint Genesius is also the Patron Saint of converts, lawyers, secretaries, and victims of torture.

Feast Day: August 25

‿ᴖ◡

Saint Joseph of Cupertino
1603–1663

Born Joseph Desa of lowly rank, he was either dismissed or refused entrance into several orders because of his seemingly dim-witted nature and clumsiness. He was later admitted into the Franciscans, where he was employed primarily in the lowly position of stable hand.

However, such was his faith that Joseph remained with the order for seventeen years until he was finally ordained in 1628. He was known for his ecstasies and miracles; among the most notable were levitations. It is said that he experienced more than seventy levitations in his life, many of which were verified by dozens of eyewitness accounts. He was witnessed several times "flying" from the back of the church, near the door, over the heads of the congregation to the altar.

He is also the Patron Saint of travelers.

Feast Day: September 18

ARCHITECTS

Saint Thomas the Apostle
  First century A.D.

Nicknamed Didymus (Greek for "twin"), he was one of the twelve Apostles and known for "doubting" Jesus' resurrection. "Unless I see . . . and touch . . . I will not believe" (John xx, 25). His doubts were vanquished when he saw for himself the risen Jesus and touched his wounds. Later, he is said to have founded a great number of churches during his journeys preaching the gospel.

He is said to have been martryed in southern India, though others have written of him preaching the gospel in Parthia, Persia, Mesopotamia, and Edessa. It is also said that his remains were taken to Edessa, then to the island of Khios, in the Aegean, and today can be found in the city of Ortona in the Abruzzi.

Saint Thomas is also the Patron Saint of those ready to marry, builders, surveyors, masons, quarrymen, carpenters, and theologians.

Feast Day: December 21

Saint Catherine of Bologna
1413–1463

Born Catherine de'Vigri, she was the handmaiden of Nicholas III d'Estes at Ferrar. She then joined the group of Franciscans who later became Poor Clare nuns. In 1456 she became the abbess of a new convent in Bologna, the convent of Corpus Christi at the behest of Pope Nicholas V.

From a very early age, she received divine visions, some of which she knew would lead her to temptation, others of a more inspirational nature. She excelled at calligraphy and painting and left behind after her death a number of poems, prose, and verse which detail her mystical visions. When she died there were reports of a heavenly aroma emanating from her body. Her incorrupt body remains at the church convent in Bologna.

Feast Day: March 9

Saint Luke
First century A.D.

A physician by profession, he became a fellow worker of Saint Paul, loyally remaining with him until the Apostle's eventual matyrdom. He is well-known for writing the Third Gospel and the Acts of the Apostles. He is said to have been a great artist in words, using them to paint the divine pictures that can be found in his written works.

He is also the Patron Saint of doctors, painters, notaries, bookbinders, lace-makers, butchers, gold-workers, bulls, and other cattle.

Feast Day: October 18

Saint Sebastian
  Died A.D. *288*

Born in Gaul, Sebastian is renowned for the untiring way in which he spread the faith.

Sebastian became a soldier in Rome's Imperial army in 283 and for five years defended and aided Christians without drawing undue attention to himself.

When it was discovered that he was a Christian, he was tied to a post and used as a target for the army's archers. However, his wounds were miraculously healed by the widow of another martyr, Saint Castulus. Upon hearing of the miracle, Diocletian ordered that he be beaten to death with clubs.

Sebastian is also the Patron Saint of soldiers, cattle, archers, marksmen, hunters, gunsmiths, invalids due to war, potters, frail children, the dying, and opponents of enemies of religion.

Feast Day: January 20

--- ᘓᐯᗇ ---

Saint Elizabeth of Hungary
1207–1231

Born in Pressburg, Hungary, she was the daughter of Andrew II of Hungary. She married royalty and bore four children. However, after the death of her husband during the Crusades, she renounced all worldly possessions and devoted herself to the sick and impoverished.

She would go on to build many hospitals in which she cared for the sick. She was the princess who cared for the sick, the aged, and the poor in what we would now call a "hospice" in Marburg, Germany. She is invoked as the patron saint of bakers because of her dedication to feeding the sick and poor in a hospital she built in Wartburg, Hungary.

It is said that in 1225 she distributed her entire supply of grain to the needy after Germany was devastated by famine.

After her death several miracles were reported at her tomb.

Saint Elizabeth is also the Patron Saint of charitable organizations, beggars, widows, orphans, innocents, and lace-makers.

Feast Day: November 17

Saint Cosmas and Saint Damian
Died circa A.D. 303

Twin Arabian brothers, both doctors, they treated the poor, practicing their profession without payment. Famed for their skills, Christian charity, and spreading the word of the Gospel, they are also credited with many miraculous healings. As their fame spread, they were ordered put to death by the Emperor Diocletian. However, they survived death by water, fire, and crucifixion before they were finally beheaded.

They are also the Patron Saints of nurses, doctors, pharmacists, the infirm, medical staffs, surgeons, the bedridden, chemists, grocers, dentists, and candy makers.

Feast Day: September 26

Saint Martín de Porres
1579–1639

Born in Lima, Peru, he was the illegitimate son of a John de Porres, a Spanish knight, and Anna, a Panamanian Indian and freed slave. At a very young age he was apprenticed to a barber and surgeon, and though he left that profession to become a Dominican lay brother, he continued to practice the crafts of hair-cutting, medicine, and what would today be called nursing. Saint Martín went on to establish both a hospital and an orphanage. He is most widely known for his compassion to the poor and those in need, including African slaves. He is also said to have shown compassion for animals, even vermin.

He is also the Patron Saint of interracial justice, nurses, health-care providers, and invoked against rats and mice.

Feast Day: November 3

Saint Stephen of Hungary (Stephen I)
  975–1038

Born into a royal family, baptized at the age of ten, he is credited with bringing order to the "Magyars," the native people of Hungary. He was given the crown by Pope Sylvester II, thus becoming the first king of Hungary. He went on tirelessly to spread the word of Christianity throughout his kingdom. He established monastaries, built churches and abbeys. Although his personal life was often turbulent, he remained a fair and kind ruler.

Saint Stephen is also the Patron Saint of horses.

Feast Day: August 16

BUSINESSWOMEN

Saint Margaret Clitherow
(also known as Saint Margaret of York)
  1556–1586

Born Margaret Middleton, she was born at York, England.
She was known as a fair and capable businesswoman who
assisted her husband in his butcher shop.

Several years into her marriage, she was converted to
Catholicism. She was imprisoned for two years for her
faith during Queen Elizabeth I's attempt to purge all Cath-
olics from England. Upon her release from prison she
again risked her life and freedom by sheltering priests in
her house. When she was caught, she was condemned
to death.

She is also the Patron Saint of converts.

Feast Day: March 25

Saint Fiacre (Fiachra)
  Died circa A.D. *670*

In Paris the taxis are known as "fiacres" because the first "coach for hire" was established in 1670 and was located near the Hotel Saint-Fiacre.

Born in Ireland, he lived alone as a hermit until granted land for a hermitage by Saint Faro of Meaux. He later built an abbey in Brueil for his disciples. He was known for his generosity toward strangers and many miraculous healings are attributed to him, particularly for those suffering from hemorrhoids.

It is said that he miraculously cleared the land surrounding the abbey by lifting his staff. It is also related that the same land later supplied an abundance of fine vegetables which he grew and fed to his guests.

He is also the Patron Saint of gardeners and is invoked by those suffering from hemorrhoids.

Feast Day: September 1

Saint Joseph
  First century A.D.

All that is known of Joseph is what is written in Matthew and Luke. He is described as a "just man." Devotion to him as a Saint has been widespread since the Middle Ages, though it was not until the papacy of Pope Pius IX that he was formally canonized.

Saint Joseph is also the Patron Saint of laborers, a good death, chastity, marriage and family, orphans, inns, those seeking shelter, refugees, and woodcutters.

Feast Days: March 19; May 1

Saint Lawrence of Rome (Lawrence the Martyr)
  Died circa A.D. *258*

The most celebrated of the Roman martyrs, Lawrence was one of the deacons of Pope Sixtus II. Lawrence renounced all worldly goods, declaring that the poor were the treasures of the church. His actions so angered the Roman emperor that he was put to death by ''roasting'' on a gridiron.

It is said that so great was his faith that he did not feel the heat, though he prayed for the conversion of Rome. However, there is some dispute as to the cause of his death. While it is commonly accepted that he was burned to death, some scholars maintain that he was beheaded, as was Sixtus. He was buried on the site of what is now the Basilica.

Saint Lawrence is also the Patron Saint of the souls in Purgatory, schoolchildren, students, administrators, the poor, librarians, and all jobs which involve fire. He is also invoked against burning, lumbago, and fevers.

Feast Day: August 10

Cooks, Housewives, and Dietitians

Saint Martha of Bethany
 First century A.D.

Sister of Mary and Saint Lazarus, she is also the Patron
Saint of housewives because she welcomed Jesus into her
house in Bethany during the course of his ministry. She
prepared the food and rest for Jesus during his stays. She
is the Patron Saint of cooks and housewives because of
her selfless service to others.

She is also the Patron Saint of housekeepers for
churches, mountain shepherds and shepherdesses, land-
lords, painters, sculptors, hospital administrators, female
laborers, and those dying of hemophilia.

Feast Day: July 29

Saint Philemon
Died A.D. 305

A famed entertainer—dancer and musician—during the reign of the Roman Emperor Diocletian, he was hired to perform a sacrificial dance to pagan gods, taking the place of deacon Apollonius. However, just before he was to perform, he was converted by the Holy Spirit and steadfastly refused to entertain in the name of pagan gods. His display of faith outraged the emperor and Saint Philemon was subsequently arrested for his crime and martyred with Apollonius by drowning.

He is also the Patron Saint of converts.

Feast Day: March 8

Saint Apollonia of Alexandria
  Died A.D. *249*

As a deaconess, she refused to renounce her faith during the reign of Emperor Philip. Although suffering brutal torture, during which her teeth were broken, she remained faithful. When finally threatened by burning, it is said that she jumped onto her own pyre rather than renounce her faith.

She is also invoked against toothaches.

Feast Day: February 9

Saint Pantaleon of Nicomedia
  Died A.D. *305*

A doctor by profession, he was the royal physician to Emperor Maximilian. However, after his conversion, he sold his possessions and provided medical treatment to the destitute, who would have otherwise gone without care.

It is said that he practiced his trade with great compassion and without payment. He was martyred by beheading under the reign of Diocletian, but only after numerous other attempts were made on his life. His name in Greek is translated as "All Compassionate."

Saint Pantaleon is also the Patron Saint of midwives, livestock, and invoked against headaches, locusts, loneliness, and accidents.

Feast Day: July 27

EDITORS

Saint John Bosco
  1815–1888

Guided by vivid divinely inspired dreams, he dedicated his life to helping the abused and homeless boys of his native Italy. He founded the Salesians in 1859.

The order's work includes schools, colleges, seminaries, adult schools, and vocational training programs, hospitals, and missions around the world. However, they are especially renowned for their printing and book production facilities.

Saint Bosco is also the Patron Saint of schoolchildren, publishing businesses, and young people in general.

Feast Day: January 31

Saint Ferdinand III
  1198–1252

The king of Castile and León, his reign was marked by almost uninterrupted crusades against the Muslims in Spain. When, in 1236, he took Savile, he founded the Cathedral of Burgos and refounded the University of Salamanca. In addition, he is credited with building countless hospitals, monasteries, churches, and cathedrals during his reign. He is regarded in all respects as a fair and just ruler.

Saint Ferdinand is also the Patron Saint of parents who have large families.

Feast Day: May 30

FARMERS

—————————————————— ⟨∿⟩ ——————————————————

Saint Isidore the Farmer (Isidore the Husbandman)
   1070–1170

The Patron Saint of farmers as well as the city of Madrid, Spain, Isidore was a pious farmhand born into poverty in his native Spain. He never owned his own land. Rather, he worked on the farm of the estate located in Torrelanguna that belonged to a wealthy businessman in Madrid.

It is said that he attended Mass each and every morning before beginning work and if his devotions made him late for his toil in the fields, angels then completed his work.

Throughout his life, he showed great charity toward the poor and unfortunate and was rewarded with miracles, such as the multiplication of food during shortages, which were common at the time. He married Saint Mary de la Cabeza. It is said that King Philip III experienced a miraculous healing at Saint Isidore's intercession.

Saint Isidore is also the Patron Saint of laborers and invoked at the death of a child.

Feast Day: May 15

Saint Florian and companions
  Died A.D. *304*

A high-ranking officer in Rome's army, he was "based" in what is now Austria. When he was touched by the spirit and announced his conversion to Christianity, he was set on fire and thrown into the River Enns. For this reason, he is said to intercede and protect against all manner of flood and fire.

Saint Florian is also the Patron Saint of smiths and brewers, and is invoked against fire, flood, storm, and infertile fields.

Feast Day: May 4

FISHERMEN

―――――――――――――――――――――― ᴄᴡᴐ ―――――

Saint Andrew the Apostle
  First century A.D.

A citizen of Bethsaida in Galilee, fisherman by trade, Andrew was the first of Christ's Apostles. He later converted his younger brother, Simon (Saint Peter). He is said to have spread the teachings of Jesus in Asia Minor and Greece. He was martyred at Patras in Achaia on an X-shaped cross. He is also the Patron Saint of Russia, Scotland, and Greece.

Saint Andrew is also the Patron Saint of fish sellers, ropemakers, butchers, spinsters, weddings, and invoked against infertility, sore throats, and gout.

Feast Day: November 30

Saint Thérèse of Lisieux
   1873–1897

Known as the "Little Flower of Jesus," she was born Marie-Françoise-Thérèse Martin to poor parents in the town of Alençon, France. After overcoming her parents' opposition, she joined the Carmelites at the age of fifteen.

Such was her devotion that her "little way" of simplicity and perfection of doing even the smallest tasks, became a model. Her autobiography, *The Story of a Soul* (also known as *Autobiography of a Saint*), which she penned at the urging of her superiors, continues to be widely read as a source of Christian inspiration throughout the world.

Since her death at age twenty-four, numerous miracles have been attributed to her intercession.

Saint Thérèse is also the Patron Saint of world missions.

Feast Day: October 1

GARDENERS

Saint Adelard
753–827

The grandson of Charles Martel and nephew of King
Pépin, he is also known for prompting his first cousin
Charlemagne to lead a more public life. He became a
monk in 773 where he was assigned as gardener. It is
said that he performed his tasks in an uncomplaining
and dedicated manner, and eventually became abbot.
He was later banished to the island of Heri for suspicion
of political betrayal, though he later returned to Corbie.

Feast Day: January 30

Saint Phocas the Gardener
Died A.D. 303

A gardener in Sinope, on the Black Sea, he performed his
work with care and dedication, while offering food and
lodging to any stranger who asked. He suffered martyrdom
under Diocletian. It is said, that Roman soldiers, sent to
find him, unknowingly accepted his hospitality. When he
learned of their mission, he dug his own grave and then
surrendered.

Feast Day: September 22

Saint Fiacre (Fiachra)
  Died circa A.D. *670*

Born in Ireland, he lived alone as a hermit until granted land for a hermitage by Saint Faro of Meaux. He later built an abbey in Brueil for his disciples. He was known for his generosity toward strangers and many miraculous healings are attributed to him, particularly from those suffering from hemorrhoids.

It is said that he miraculously cleared the land surrounding the abbey by lifting his staff. It is also related that the same land later supplied an abundance of fine vegetables, which he grew and fed to his guests.

Also the Patron Saint of taxi drivers. In Paris the taxis are known as "fiacres," because the first "coach for hire" was established in 1670 and was located near the Hotel Saint-Fiacre. He is also invoked by those suffering from hemorrhoids.

Feast Day: September 1

Saint Martha of Bethany
First century A.D.

Sister of Mary and Saint Lazarus, she is also the Patron
Saint of housewives because she welcomed Jesus into her
house in Bethany during the course of his ministry. She
prepared the food and rest for Jesus during his stays. She
is the Patron Saint of cooks and housewives because of
her selfless service to others.

She is also the Patron Saint of housekeepers for
churches, mountain shepherds and shepherdesses, land-
lords, painters, sculptors, hospital administrators, female
laborers, and those dying of hemophilia.

Feast Day: July 29

Armand (Almandus of Elnon)
584–679

Born in Bourges, France, Amand began his religious life
as a hermit and was later consecrated a bishop. He became
a legendary missionary and founded several monasteries
throughout what is today Belgium and France, monasteries
which were known for their hospitality. He is most often
shown in art as holding a church in his hand.

Saint Amand is also the Patron Saint of wine merchants.

Feast Day: February 6

Saint Dunstan
910–988

The most prominent Anglo-Saxon Saint. During his lifetime, he was an abbot, archbishop, and political adviser to English royalty. He was also famed for his goldsmithing, tapestries, music, and manuscript artwork, called illumination. During his lifetime, he initiated reform in the English churches. He was appointed papal legate in 961 by Pope John XII.

Saint Dustan is also the Patron Saint of goldsmiths, armorers, and blacksmiths.

Feast Day: May 19

Saint Eligius of Noyon (Éloi or Eloy)
588–660

Born in Limoges, France, he was a master metalworker and smith. Appointed master of the mint in Paris by the king at the time, King Clotaire II, he grew in political influence. Later he was ordained bishop of Noyon and founded the Solignac abbey and other convents and monasteries.

Also the patron saint of metalworkers, farmers, miners, armorers, clockmakers, engravers, lamp makers, horses, horse dealers, basket makers, and tenant farmers.

Feast Day: December 1

Saint Nicholas of Flüe (Nicholas von der Flüe)
   1417–1487

Born in Switzerland, he was the son of a peasant farmer. After exhibiting bravery on the battlefield, he was appointed a judge. At the age of fifty, he left his family, which included ten children, and lived as a hermit for nearly twenty years.

His advice was much prized by those who visited him, particularly by those involved in the field of law. He is still much admired in Switzerland as a patriot as well as a Saint.

He is also the Patron Saint of Switzerland and that country's first "national" Patron Saint.

Feast Day: March 27

Saint Ivo of Kermartin
(Ivo [Yvo] Helory or Saint Ivo of Brittany)
  1253–1303

The son of a nobleman, Ivo immersed himself in the study of law, philosophy, and religion in Paris and Orléans. When he returned home to his native city in Brittany, near Treguier, he practiced law in both religious and civil courts.

He eventually became known as a lawyer who would apply his formidable skills as advocate for the poor and needy as well as the wealthy. He later used the fees he accepted from wealthy clients to build a hospital.

The last fifteen years of his life, he spent not in the law, but rather devoted to parish work.

Saint Ivo is also the Patron Saint of the poor, court ushers (today bailiffs), notaries, priests, parish priests, orphans during trials, and is a symbol of virtue and equality before the law.

Feast Day: May 19

Saint Thomas More
  1478–1535

Perhaps the most famous of the English Saints, Thomas More was born in London. He received a legal degree from Oxford and served as chancellor under King Henry

VIII. He was elected Lord Chancellor in 1511. He gained fame in his time by his writings, which included both political and religious works. When he refused to renounce the supremacy of the papacy, King Henry VIII accused him of treason and had him imprisoned. After more than a year in prison, he was beheaded.

Saint Thomas More is also the Patron Saint of parents with large families, stepparents, widowers, and ''hard'' marriages.

Feast Day: June 22

Saint Jerome
  342–420

Saint Jerome was born at Stridon, but studied in Rome, becoming well versed in Greek, Latin, and all of the classical writers. After seeing Christ in a vision, he was converted to Christianity and became a hermit in Syria for four years. When he returned to Rome and his ordination, he became secretary to the Pope.

Saint Jerome would later return to the Middle East to live out his remaining days, but not before founding a monastary and several convents. He translated the Bible from its original Hebrew and Greek to Latin, which became the official text for the Catholic Church.

Saint Jerome is also the Patron Saint of girls' reformatories, orphanages, and the founders of schools.

Feast Day: September 30

MAIDS AND SERVANTS

--- ᜑ ---

Saint Zita
  1218–1272

Born in Monsagrati, Italy, she entered the service of a
wealthy family at age twelve. Devoted to Christianity from
an early age, she attended Mass each morning before beginning work. This unwavering devotion, along with her
habit of giving food and clothing to the poor, at first only
earned her the wrath of both her employer and fellow
servants. Yet, as time passed, both came to understand the
divine nature of her holiness.

Several miracles, as well as the multiplication of food,
are attributed to her. She remained in the service of the
family for her entire life, becoming a favorite among the
children.

Saint Zita is also the Patron Saint of single women.

Feast Day: April 27

Saint Francis of Assisi
  1182–1226

One of the most beloved of all the Saints, Francis of Assisi, Italy, was born the son of a wealthy merchant. Following a youth spent enjoying worldly pleasures, he founded the order of Friars Minor in 1209, which pledged chastity, obedience, and poverty. The order soon grew in popularity, despite setbacks and internal problems.

After an unsuccessful trip to the Middle East to convert Muslims, Francis was imprinted with the Passion of the stigmata, the first recorded instance of this heavenly phenomenon.

Saint Francis is also the Patron Saint of the blind, the lame, prisoners, cloth merchants, cloth traders, social workers, weavers, and environmentalists.

Feast Day: October 4

Saint Cecilia
  Second century A.D.

One of the earliest Roman martyrs, she was married against her will, though she convinced her husband Saint Valerian to let her retain her virginity and to live as a Christian.

During her lifetime she was widely recognized for her charitable works, though the reason behind her being the Patron Saint of musicians remains clouded to this day. It is said that she was executed by a Roman soldier, who in failing to behead her, inflicted a mortal wound from which she bled to death after three days of suffering.

Saint Cecilia is also the Patron Saint of church music, choir members, poets, and those who make or build instruments.

Feast Day: November 22

Saint Gregory the Great
  540–604

Born in Rome to wealthy parents, he held high political office in that city. However, upon resigning the office, he turned his home into a monastery and became a monk.

Saint Gregory was later one of the first monks to become Pope and in that office became one of the great figures in world history. In one instance, he sent Saint Augustine to England to convert the Saxons and later spread the word among all of Western Europe. He is known as the Patron Saint of musicians for the influence he had on Church liturgical music.

Also the Patron Saint of teachers, pupils, schools, music schools, singers, masons, and learned men.

Feast Day: September 3

PAINTERS

Saint Luke the Evangelist
First century A.D.

A Greek doctor, he worked with Saint Paul and remained with him until the martyr's death. He is also the author of the Third Gospel and the Acts of the Apostles.

One story attributes to him seven portraits of the Virgin after speaking with her. Another places him as the Patron Saint of artists because of the "graphic" style of his writing.

Saint Luke is also the Patron Saint of doctors, bookbinders, butchers, lace-makers, bulls, cattle, gold-workers, notaries, and sculptors.

Feast Day: October 18

Saint Gemma Galgani
  1878–1903

Born in Tuscany, Italy, she lost her mother when she was seven years old. Her life was an almost unbroken chain of suffering, not the least of which was a physical infirmity of the spine that prevented her from becoming a nun.

However, despite her ordeals, she remained a strong believer. Later, she was blessed with a variety of spiritual occurrences, including a recurring stigmata.

Feast Day: April 11

―――――――――――――――――――――― ᏬᏉ ―――

Saint Michael the Archangel

The Patron Saint of police officers as well as soldiers, he is one of the three archangels mentioned in the Bible and one of the seven angels who stand before God's throne. Michael is often seen as a protector and described as the "chief" prince and the one who leads the army of God into battle against hell's evil.

Saint Michael is also the Patron Saint of those who make or adjust scales, merchants who use a scale, bakers, painters, soldiers, tailors, and churchyards. He is also invoked for a good death and against lightning storms.

Feast Day: September 29

Saint Gabriel the Archangel

One of the three archangels, Gabriel appeared to the Virgin Mary to tell her that she would give birth to the Savior. He was also the angel who convinced Joseph that he should marry Mary and warned him of Herod's plan to kill all infants in a vain attempt to kill Jesus. The name Gabriel means "messenger."

Saint Gabriel is also the Patron Saint of stamp collectors, news organizations, and radio and television employees.

Feast Day: September 29

Saint Bernardino of Siena
 1380–1444

Born in Mass Marittima, Italy, to a prominent family, he was orphaned young and later entered the Franciscan order. In his time he was seen as the leading missionary, preaching his entire life and thus creating a multitude of believers and reform within the church.

Saint Bernardino is also the Patron Saint of wool weavers, and invoked against chest pains, sickness, and bleeding.

Feast Day: May 20

Saint Joan of Arc
  1412–1431

Also the Patron Saint of soldiers because of her military skills in the name of Christianity, she is seen as the Patron Saint of television and radio workers because of the divine voices that showed her the way in her faith.

She was born into the family of a peasant farmer in France. She began hearing voices while still a teenager. At seventeen, she persuaded King Charles VII to allow her to lead his army against the English. After a series of decisive victories, she was captured and handed over to the British. It was decided before a corrupt ecclesiastical court that the visions and voices she received were not divine, but evil, and she was burned at the stake.

In 1456, twenty-five years after her death, another court declared her innocent of the charges. She was canonized in 1920. It is important to remember that she was canonized as a Holy Maiden and not a martyr.

Feast Day: May 30

Saint Albert the Great
  1200–1280

He entered the order of Dominicans and taught Saint Thomas Aquinas and later went on to serve as bishop. Perhaps one of the church's greatest men of science, he was well versed in biology, chemistry, physics, mathematics, astronomy, and geography. Educated at the University of Padua, he was also expert in philosophy and theology.

   Saint Albert is also the Patron Saint of all medical technicians, such as those involved in radiology.

Feast Day: November 15

Saint Genesius (Gene) of Arles
  Died A.D. *303*

This French Saint was the town's notary and official "shorthand" writer. He was martyred by Maximilan Herculeus when he refused to record an official decree against Christians.

Saint Genesius is also the Patron Saint of comedians, converts, lawyers, and victims of torture.

Feast Day: August 25

Saint Louise de Marillac
  1591–1660

A native Parisian, she was steered away from religious duty at an early age by her priest. She went on to marry, though after the death of her husband, she devoted her life to Christ. She worked with Saint Vincent de Paul to establish the Sisters of Charity in 1638. She went on to establish nearly fifty orders throughout France.

Feast Day: March 15

Saint George (George the Great)
  Died A.D. *303 or 305*

In truth, relatively little is known for fact about Saint George, though most scholars agree he was a martyr who suffered his death at the behest of Diospolis in what was then called Palestine. The most popular story attributed to him is the one in which he killed a dragon to free the people of a city in what is now called Libya. It is also said that he was a soldier in the army of Emperor Constantine.

Saint George is also the Patron Saint of crusaders, peasants, working animals, horses, and England. He is invoked against plague, leprosy, syphilis, and snakebite.

Feast Day: April 23

Saint Hadrian (Adrian) Nicomedia
  Died A.D. *304*

A soldier in Nicomedia's pagan army, he was imprisoned for showing compassion to Christians at the sight of the faithful being tortured for their devotion to God.

While he was in prison, his wife, Saint Natalia, showed devotion in her attention to her husband and his fellow prisoners. After his torture and execution, Natalia fled to what is now Turkey.

Saint Hadrian is also the Patron Saint of prison guards, messengers, and invoked in cases of sudden death.

Feast Day: September 8

Saint Ignatius of Loyola
1491–1556

Born of a wealthy family in Spain, the youngest of thirteen children, he entered the military seeking his fame. However, when he was wounded in a battle against France, he began his study of the Scriptures. Gathering around him a small band of nine men, he formed the Society of Jesus (Jesuits), devoted to obedience to the Church and the Pope. At the end of his life, the nine companions had grown to thousands and he had founded schools, colleges, and seminaries.

Saint Ignatius is also the Patron Saint of expectant mothers, children, and invoked to improve scruples.

Feast Day: March 15

Saint Martin of Tours
316–397

The son of a Roman army officer, he was conscripted into the army against his will. He later refused to fight against the Germans because he felt that Christians should not pursue war. It is said that on encountering a beggar, he tore his cloak in half to offer the poor man some comfort, at which time the beggar revealed himself as Jesus. He then left the army and became a hermit and later established monasteries.

Saint Martin is also the Patron Saint of riders, blacksmiths, armorers, weavers, tailors, beggars, prisoners, and vintners.

Feast Day: November 11

Saint Homobonus
  Died 1197

Born into a wealthy merchant family in Italy, he went on to conduct a successful clothing business himself. However, it is said that he was fair in all of his dealings and gave most of his fortune away to the needy. He was a devoted Christian who praised God for both his talent with needle and thread as well as his good fortune in business.

Feast Day: November 13

Saint Gregory the Great
  540–604

The first monk to become Pope, he was born in Rome to wealthy parents. He held high political office in that city. However, upon resigning the office, he turned his home into a monastery and became a monk. As Pope he became one of the great figures in world history. In one instance, he sent Saint Augustine to England to convert the Saxons and later spread the word among all of Western Europe.

He is known as the Patron Saint of musicians for the influence he had on Church liturgical music as well as the Patron Saint of pupils, schools, music schools, singers, masons, and learned men.

Feast Day: September 3

Saint John Baptiste de la Salle
  1651–1719

Born in France, he was ordained in 1678 and dedicated his life to serving the Lord through the education of young people. Many of today's most basic educational concepts can be credited to him. Many educational theories he developed were later adopted by the Brothers of the Christian Schools, which he founded. Among his ideas for the reform of educational study was the concept of the classroom, as opposed to individual study that was the norm during his time.

He is also the Patron Saint of schools for the poor.

Feast Day: April 7

Saint Francis de Sales
    1567–1622

In addition to founding the Order of the Visitation as well as numerous schools, his prolific spiritual writings, such as *Introduction to a Devout Life,* outlined and taught that spiritual perfection is attainable for every Christian.

Saint Francis is also the Patron Saint of authors of all sorts, as well as the Catholic press.

Feast Day: January 24

Words of Divine Wisdom

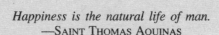

Happiness is the natural life of man.
—SAINT THOMAS AQUINAS

*Men travel to wonder at the height of mountains, at
the huge waves of the sea, at the long courses of
the rivers, at the vast compass of the ocean, at the
circular motion of the stars. And they pass
by themselves without wondering.*
—SAINT AUGUSTINE

Laugh and grow strong.
—SAINT IGNATIUS OF LOYOLA

*Laugh and play and dash about as much as you like,
only be careful not to say or do anything that would
be displeasing to God.*
—SAINT MARY MAZZARELLO

Astronomy

Saint Dominic de Guzmán (Dominic of Caleruega) 1170–1221

Born in Spain, Dominic is best known for his tireless work in conversions throughout Europe. He founded the Order of Preachers (Dominicans) with six followers in France. It is also said that he raised a cardinal's nephew from the dead. He died in extreme poverty.

He is also the Patron Saint of tailors and invoked against fever.

Feast Day: August 8

Saint Adjuter (Ayutre)
Died 1131

He was a Norman knight who sailed off in the first Crusade, but was captured by Muslims. Upon his escape, he returned to France and entered the abbey in Tiron, though he later left to become a hermit.

Feast Day: April 30

Saint Eustachius
Died A.D. 118

Born into a prominent Roman family, he was converted when he saw a divine vision of a stag with a crucifix between its antlers. He was later martyred along with his family by Hadrian.

He is also the Patron Saint of helpers in time of need, foresters, grocers, and merchants who deal in clothing or cloth.

Feast Day: September 20

Saint Hubert of Liège
Died A.D. 727

A courtier in France, who in the midst of mourning his wife saw a divine vision while hunting. Henceforth, he devoted his life in the service of the Lord. He succeeded Saint Lambert as bishop of Maestricht.

Saint Hubert is also the Patron Saint of manufacturers, computer programmers, butchers, opticians, hunting dogs, and invoked against dog bites and rabies.

Feast Day: May 30

Saint Bernard of Montjoux
Died 1081

As a vicar he tirelessly visited the faithful in even the remote Alpine valleys of his parish.

Saint Bernard is also the Patron Saint of skiers and snowboarders.

Feast Day: May 28

Saint Lydwin (Lydwina) of Schiedam
1380–1433

Born into a modest family, she suffered a minor accident while ice skating at age sixteen. However, complications soon compounded her woes and she became bedridden for the remainder of her life with painful illnesses.

She suffered with patience and immersed herself in prayer and devotion. After years in bed, she began to experience divine visions.

She is also the Patron Saint of those suffering with sickness, particularly those who are bedridden.

Feast Day: April 14

Saint Bernard of Montjoux
Died 1081

Also the Patron Saint of mountain and rock climbers, as a vicar, he tirelessly visited the faithful in even the remote Alpine valleys of his parish.

Feast Day: May 28

Saint Anthony (Antony) of Padua
1195–1231

Certainly one of the most popular saints, he is also often invoked in the search for lost objects. Originally a native of Lisbon, he entered the Canons Regular when he was young, but left a few years later for the Friars Minor in Coimbra. After an unsuccessful attempt to journey to Africa in order to spread the word, he went to Italy. There, under the direction of Saint Francis, he began preaching with much success. It is said that shopkeepers and businessmen left their places of work in order to hear his sermons.

Saint Anthony is also the Patron Saint of those in love, married couples, women, children, horses, donkeys, travelers, and invoked against fever, infertility, shipwreck, and war.

Feast Day: June 13

Words of Divine Wisdom

What is nobler than to mold the character of the young?
I consider that he who knows how to form the youthful mind is truly greater than all painters, sculptors and
all others of that sort.
—SAINT JOHN CHRYSOSTOM

For those in the married state, the best example we
can cite is that of Saint Joachim and Saint Anne,
who every year divided their income into three equal
parts. One was for the poor, the second for the temple and the fine service, and the third for themselves.
—SAINT IGNATIUS OF LOYOLA

You can do nothing with children unless you win their
confidence and love by bringing them into touch
with oneself, by breaking through all the hindrances
that keep them at a distance. We must
accommodate ourself to their tastes, we must
make ourselves like them.
—SAINT JOHN BOSCO

... even as thou seekest a virtuous, fair, good spouse,
so think likewise how she would fain have a husband
prudent, discreet, good, and fulfilled of all virtue.
—SAINT HUGH OF LINCOLN

Guard your tongue when your husband is angry.
—SAINT MONICA

In three different ways a woman can fulfill the mission
of motherliness: in marriage, in the practice of a

profession which values human development . . . and under the veil as the spouse of Christ.
—SAINT THERESIA BENEDICTA

Being a wife and a mother was never an obstacle to my spiritual life . . . I have been very happy with my husband.
—SAINT CONCEPCION CABRERA DE ARMIDA

No one heals himself by wounding another.
—SAINT AMBROSE

Disorder in society is the result of disorder in the family.
—SAINT ANGELA MERICI

Purity? They ask. And they smile. They are the very people who approach marriage with worn-out bodies and disillusioned minds.
—VENERABLE JOSÉ ESCRIVÁ

CHILDBIRTH WITHOUT PAIN

Saint Hyacinth of Cracow
  Died 1257

Born of noble parents, he entered the Dominican order and became an active missionary throughout Eastern Europe. Numerous miracles are attributed to him, including the raising of a drowned child and walking on water. It is also said that he restored sight to a pair of blind twins and saved many people when a bridge they were crossing collapsed.

He is also invoked against the dangers of drowning.

Feast Day: August 17

Saint Nicholas of Myra
Died A.D. 350

Perhaps the most well known of all the Saints among children, Saint Nick, as he is called, was the bishop of Myra in Lycia. Several stories surround his legend, the first being how he rescued three children who had been cruelly pickled in brine. The legend of his gift giving derives from a tale in which he heard of a man who had no dowry for his three daughters. Saint Nick eased the problem by anonymously leaving a bag of gold in the man's house. It is said that he later did the same for other girls.

He is also the Patron Saint of lawyers, pharmacists, ribbon makers, farmers, beer manufacturers, fishermen, fish sellers, prisoners, young women, children, butchers, notaries, perfume sales people, distillers, pawnbrokers, seamen, cloth merchants, wine merchants, hotel managers, and helpers in time of need.

The name "Santa Claus" derives from the Dutch pronunciation "Sin Klaes."

Feast Day: December 6

Saint Firmin of Amiens (Firminus I)
Died fourth century A.D.

Born in Spain, he was educated by Saint Honestus and consecrated bishop of Amiens. A missionary bishop, many miracles are attributed to him, including the healing of the sick and restoration of sight to the blind. He was eventually imprisoned and martyred for his faith in Christ.

Firmin is also the Patron Saint of wine merchants and bakers.

Feast Day: September 25

Saint Agnes of Rome
Died A.D. 304

Born of a noble family in Rome, she refused marriage at a very young age—twelve or thirteen—and swore a vow of chastity. When the persecutions began under Diocletian, she was martyred. Pope Saint Damasus himself wrote her epitaph and her name occurs in the canon at Mass. She is also a special Patron Saint of chastity.

One of the most popular of all Saints, several stories exist of miraculous occurrences. It is said that she was brought unclothed to a house of ill repute in order to break down her resolve to follow Christ, but a coat of hair grew on her body to cover her. It is also said that when her spurned fiancé touched her body, he immediately died. And when Agnes pleaded to God to bring him back to life, he recovered.

She is also the Patron Saint of virgins, children, and gardeners.

Feast Day: January 21

Saint Anne
First century A.D.

Anne or Hannah, means "grace." She gave birth to the Blessed Virgin Mary at age forty. Supposedly barren, a heavenly angel appeared to her and told Anne that she would have a child. She then promised to dedicate the child to God.

Saint Anne is also the Patron Saint of widows, pregnant women, nannies, bridal couples, household items, tailors, grocers, ropemakers, lace-makers, and the dying.

Feast Day: July 26

Saint Wolfgang of Regensburg
  Died A.D. *994*

A Benedictine monk and a bishop, he spent his life dedicated to teaching and missionary work. Many miracles and divinely inspired deeds are related about his life.

It is said that he cured a knight even after the knight defamed him; that when he leaned against a rock with outstretched arms, he left the impression of a cross in the stone; and that when he was conceived, it felt to his mother as if she were carrying "a star."

Saint Wolfgang is also the Patron Saint of lumberjacks, sailors, and invoked against lameness, gout, stroke, and dysentery.

Feast Day: October 31

Saint Colman of Melk
  Died 1012

Irish by birth, during his pilgrimage in 1012, he was un-justly accused of being a Hungarian spy, arrested, and put to death. It is said that after he was hanged, his body did not show signs of decomposing for more than two years.

He is also invoked against headaches, the plague, and rain.

Feast Day: October 13

Saint Monica of Tagaste
332–387

The Christian wife of a pagan husband, she waited patiently for the conversion of her eldest son, Augustine. Through patience and kindness, she finally converted her husband, and then after his death, her son. She died the same year as his conversion, while he went on to become Saint Augustine.

She is also the Patron Saint of women.

Feast Day: August 27

Saint Dorothy of Caesarea
Dates unknown

During the persecutions under the Emperor Diocletian, Dorothy was imprisoned because she refused to marry a nobleman, having devoted herself to Christ. After many tortures which left her unharmed, she was sentenced to be beheaded, but declared that she would happily accept any suffering that brought her to the garden of her Lord. Hearing her statement of devotion, a lawyer mocked her, asking Dorothy to send him "a basket of apples and roses" when she arrived at the heavenly garden. Miraculously, after her death the lawyer received a basket of apples and roses. He was instantly converted, then very shortly thereafter put to death by the emperor.

Saint Dorothy is also the Patron Saint of florists and brewers, as well as women resting after childbirth.

Feast Day: February 6

Saint Judoc
Died A.D. *668*

Born a prince like his older brother, Saint Judicael, Judoc rejected the trappings of wealth and prestige to make his pilgrimage. It is said that along the way the animals he fed became tame. It is also said that Christ appeared to him three times disguised as a beggar, and each time Judoc shared what meager food he had with him.

In addition to being the Patron Saint of parents, he is also the Patron Saint of pets, the blessing of children, harvests, and invoked against fire, insects, and fever.

Feast Day: December 13

Saint Adalbad of Ostrevant
Died circa A.D. 652

A devoted Christian and grandson of Saint Gertrude of Hamage, he worked in the court of nobility. When he married a "Gascon girl" (Rictrudis) they lived together as good Christians. However, years following their marriage and birth of four children, her family still disapproved of him. Sixteen years after their marriage, he was lured to a secluded place and murdered by members of his wife's family. His wife, following her death, was also canonized.

Feast Day: February 2

Saint Adelaide
930–999

The daughter of the king of Burgundy, France, she married Lothair II of Italy. However, following his death, she had to endure many hardships at the hands of in-laws and even her own son and daughter-in-law. Throughout her hardships, she consistently found comfort in the act of worship and the kindness of the clergy. Her marriage to Otto I of Germany produced five children. All told she bore eight children through her two marriages, as well as adopting another.

Saint Adelaide is also the Patron Saint of widows, stepparents, young brides, and prisoners.

Feast Day: December 16

Saint Ferdinand III
1199–1252

The king of France, he fathered seven sons by his first wife, Beatrice, the daughter of the king of Swabia. Following her death, he remarried Joan of Ponthieu, with whom he had two more sons, as well as a daughter.

Saint Ferdinand is also the Patron Saint of engineers.

Feast Day: May 30

Saint Leopold (Leopold the Good)
1073–1136

Born in Austria, he married the Imperial Princess Agnes following the death of her husband. He went on to rule justly and kindly as well as to father eighteen children.

He is also the Patron Saint of stepparents and invoked in the occurrence of the death of a child.

Feast Day: November 15

Saint Margaret of Scotland
1045–1093

Married King Malcolm Canmore (Malcolm III) of Scotland and set a shining example for her people in her Christian devotion. In all, she had eight children, one of which became "Good Queen Maud," the wife of Henry I.

She is also the Patron Saint of widows and invoked in the occurrence of the death of a child.

Feast Day: November 16

Saint Thomas More
1478–1535

Even if he had not opposed Henry VIII, king of England, it is said that More would still be a candidate for sainthood. However, in addition to the inspiring story of his political life, he married Jane Holt and fathered four children. Following her death, he married Alice Middleton, who raised his children as if they were her own.

He is also the Patron Saint of lawyers as well as the Patron Saint of stepparents.

Feast Day: June 22

Saint Vladimir
956–1015

The Grand Duke of Kiev (Russia), he was married to five women on whom he fathered numerous children. However, following his conversion, he married the sister of the Greek Emperor Basil II, setting aside his previous wives.

He is also the Patron Saint of those converted to the faith as well as murderers.

Feast Day: July 15

Saint Gerard Majella
  1725–1755

Born in southern Italy, he was apprenticed to a tailor at
an early age. When he was twenty-three he entered the
order of the Redemptionists. In addition to leading an ex-
emplary life, several miracles, including multiplying food,
healing, bilocations, and prophecies are attributed to him.
He returned home later in life to care for his mother and
sisters. It is unclear just exactly why he is the Patron Saint
of expectant mothers, though some speculate it is for his
devotion to his mother.

Feast Day: October 16

Saint Leonard of Noblac
Died A.D. 550

Leonard was of noble birth, so it's odd that he is also the Patron Saint of prisoners. Well educated, he helped deliver the Frankish king's child while the king was away hunting. When asked what he wanted as reward for performing a midwife's duties, Leonard requested a plot of land on which he could devote himself to God away from worldly distractions.

He is also the Patron Saint of farmers, miners, and locksmiths.

Feast Day: November 6

Saint Catherine of Alexandria
Born circa A.D. 300

Born of royalty, highly educated and beautiful, Catherine was converted to Christ by a vision following her parents' deaths. Then, after a hermit revealed Christ to her as her bridegroom, she refused proposals of marriage by all suitors. As her devotion grew, she protested the worship of pagan idols to the Emperor Maxentius. In order to refute her claims, the emperor summoned fifty of his greatest pagan philosophers, whose arguments she neatly dispatched, then converted them before the emperor had them put to death.

It is said that after the Emperor had her killed, Saint Catherine's body bled milk and angels carried it to Mount Sinai.

She is also the Patron Saint of mothers suffering for lack of milk, nursing mothers, and invoked against diseases of the head and tongue.

Feast Day: November 25

Words of Divine Wisdom

Live in faith and hope, though it be in darkness, for in this darkness God protects the soul. Cast your care upon God for you are His and He will not forget you. Do not think that he is leaving you alone, for that would be to wrong him.
—SAINT JOHN OF THE CROSS

God measures our affliction to our need.
—SAINT JOHN CHRYSOSTOM

The prayer of a sick person is his patience and his acceptance of the sickness for the love of Jesus Christ.
—SAINT CHARLES OF SEZZE

Receive the accidents that befall thee as good, knowing that nothing happens without God.
—TEACHINGS OF THE TWELVE APOSTLES

If God causes you to suffer much, it is a sign that He has great designs for you, and that He certainly intends to make you a Saint.
—SAINT IGNATIUS LOYOLA

Make sickness itself a prayer.
—SAINT FRANCIS DE SALES

If we have any natural defect, either in mind or body, let us not grieve and be sorry for ourselves. Who is there that ever receives a gift and tries to make bargains about it? Let us, then, return thanks for what He has bestowed on us. Who can tell whether, if we had

had a larger share of ability or stronger health, we should not have possessed them to our destruction.
—SAINT ALPHONSUS LIGUORI

Many would be willing to have afflictions provided that they be not inconvenienced by them ... Suffer and offer up those trifling injuries, those petty inconveniences, that daily befall you. This toothache, this headache, this cold, this contempt or scorn.
—SAINT FRANCIS DE SALES

As too great care for bodily things is reprehensible, so reasonable care is to be commended to preserve health for the service of God.
—SAINT IGNATIUS LOYOLA

✑ILMENTS OF THE FEET

Saint John the Apostle
First century A.D.

The favorite disciple of Jesus, he was a fisherman and the brother of Saint James the Greater. Jesus asked him to care for his mother after his death. He is also the only apostle who was not a martyr.

He is also the Patron Saint of writers, and invoked against an assortment of ailments, including burns, epilepsy, and poisoning.

Feast Day: December 27

Saint Servatius
Died A.D. *384*

A bishop in what is today Belgium, it is said that he was the grandchild of Saint Anne and a member of the Holy Family. Further, it is said that he was taken prisoner by Attila the Hun, but protected by an eagle when he fell asleep and so, seeing this miracle, Attila was converted. There is also a story that he was martyred by having "clogs" (shoes) thrown at him.

He is also the Patron Saint of metalworkers and invoked against frost damage, fever, swine disease, and lameness.

Feast Day: May 13

Saint Lucy (Lucia)
Died circa A.D. 304

Named in the canon of the Mass Lucia, she was born of wealthy parents in Syracuse, Greece. Many stories surround her life. It is said that she was spurned by a suitor who discovered that she was Christian. It is also said that she was discovered in a brothel. Another story has it that she tore out her own eyes when a suitor she disliked admired them, though they were miraculously restored.

She is also the Patron Saint of former prostitutes, farmers, notaries, writers, weavers, and invoked against sore throats and infection.

Feast Day: December 13

Saint Aloysius Gonzaga
1568–1591

The oldest of thirteen children, he was born into a peasant family, but obtained a job in the royal court as a page. When he was ordered to kiss a woman's shadow, he refused, and fled the court. After receiving a vision of his death, he joined the Jesuits and died after caring for plague victims.

He is also the Patron Saint of young students.

Feast Day: June 21

Saint Louis of France (Louis IX)
1214–1270

In addition to being the Patron Saint against blindness, he is also the Patron Saint guarding against hearing loss. Louis became king of France when he was eleven. He is said to have been indifferent to the trappings of the royal court, but devoted to his wife and eleven children. He went on two Crusades, on the first of which he was captured and ransomed back to his country. During the second Crusade, he contracted typhus and died in Tunis.

He is also the Patron Saint of scientists, barbers, hairdressers, the blind, bakers, builders, printers, bookbinders, fishermen, plasterers, button makers, linen makers, quarrymen, wallpaperers, carpenters, and invoked against loss of hearing.

Feast Day: August 25

Saint Sigismund of Burgundy
Died A.D. *524*

The king of Burgundy, France, he had one son put to death by strangulation for hostility toward his stepmother. However, in remorse for his crime, he founded a monastery and entered it as a monk. It was said that he was imbued with a divinely inspired "perpetual chant." After his army's defeat, he was found in the monastery in a monk's habit and drowned in a well along with members of his family.

He is also the Patron Saint against fevers.

Feast Day: May 1

Saint Stanislas (Stanislaus) Kostka
1550–1568

The son of a powerful Polish "senator," he devoted his life early to the church and entered the Jesuits at the age of seventeen. It is said that he endured many hardships in his study, yet persevered. Legends tell us he cured a lame man and saved a young boy who fell into a well. It was reported that he received communion from angels. He died at the young age of eighteen. After his death, the town of Lublin was released from the grip of the plague.

He is also the Patron Saint of students, and invoked against fever and eye ailments.

Feast Day: November 13

Saint Thibault (Theobald) of Provence
1017–1066

The son of a count, he refused to serve in the army and left his home in France with a companion on a pilgrimage to Rome. The two earned their way by working at menial jobs and as stonemasons as well as builders. He finally settled down as a hermit in a Camaldolite monastery in Italy. It is said that he resisted many temptations and at one point was physically restrained by Satan from kneeling before a statue of Saint James in Compostela.

He is also the Patron Saint of eye diseases, ''spells of fear,'' and infertility.

Feast Day: June 30

Saint Agatha of Catania
Dates unknown

After refusing the proposal of marriage by a city official in her native Sicily, she was arrested and given over to a house of ill repute. However, she maintained her chastity and faith despite torture. It is said that she underwent many horrendous tortures, one of which was having her breasts cut off. It is also said that Saint Peter appeared to her in prison and healed her wounds before her death.

She is also the Patron Saint of nursing mothers, goldsmiths, miners, the hungry, and invoked against volcanic eruptions, fire, and earthquakes.

Feast Day: February 5

Saint Louis of France (Louis IX)
1214–1270

Also the Patron Saint guarding against blindness, he became king of France when he was eleven. He is said to have been indifferent to the trappings of the royal court, but devoted to his wife and eleven children. He went on two Crusades, on the first of which he was captured and ransomed back to his country. During the second Crusade, he contracted typhus and died in Tunis.

He is also the Patron Saint of scientists, barbers, hairdressers, the blind, bakers, builders, printers, bookbinders, fishermen, plasterers, button makers, linen makers, quarrymen, wallpaperers, and carpenters.

Feast Day: August 25

Saint Geneviève of Paris
422–500

The Patron Saint of Paris, she was inspired in her faith as a young girl. As she began spending more and more time in church, her mother tried to stop her, striking the young Geneviève. The mother was herself struck blind, but cured when her daughter brought her water, that she herself had blessed. Most of Geneviève's life was spent in service to the poor. During a war, she helped to raise the spirits of the people. It is said that her prayers also brought rain and that when there was insufficient wine for services, her prayers refilled the vessel.

She is also the Patron Saint of makers of wall coverings, vintners, and invoked against danger from fire, fever, misfortune, and for good weather and rain.

Feast Day: January 3

Saint Apollinaris of Ravenna
Died A.D. 75

The first bishop, it is said that he accompanied Saint Peter from Antioch to Rome. Many miracles are attributed to him, including curing the sick and reviving the dead. After being imprisoned, he was fed by angels and later escaped. However, after he returned to Ravenna, he was killed.

He is also the Patron Saint of needleworkers, and invoked against gallstones, epilepsy, and gout.

Feast Day: July 23

Saint Alexis (Alexius)
Died circa A.D. 400

The son of a wealthy and influential Roman, he left his bride on their wedding night to begin a pilgrimage to the Holy Land. Throughout his travels, he became famed for his devotion to the faith and his shining spirit. When he eventually returned home, he did so unrecognized, in the rags of a beggar. He lived there unnoticed on his father's estate.

Saint Alexis is also the Patron Saint of beggars, the homeless, the sick, and invoked against earthquakes, lightning, and bad weather.

Feast Day: July 17

Saint Damasus I (Damascus)
305–384

His life was marked by controversy involving the Christian politics of the day. At one time he was falsely accused of murder, but later found innocent. Became Pope in 366. During his time as Pope, he increased the prestige of Rome and persuaded followers to study Saint Jerome's writings. He composed many inscriptions for tombs and monuments which survive to this day.

Feast Day: December 11

Saint Domitian
Died A.D. 560

The bishop of Maestricht, Germany, his relics are today still venerated at Huy.

Feast Day: May 7

Saint Peter Chrysologus
  406–450

Born in Imola, he became a bishop famed for his gift of speech. Indeed, his name, ''Chrysologus,'' means ''Gold Tongue.'' Almost all that is known about him and his unwavering faith is to be found in the nearly two hundred of his sermons which have survived the years.

Feast Day: July 30

Saint Alphais
Died 1211

Born to a peasant family in Cudot, France. As a child she was inflicted with leprosy that resulted in the loss of her limbs. Although bedridden, intercession by the Virgin Mary was said to have cured her of leprosy. She is said to have had the gift of inedia, the ability to live entirely on the Eucharist. She made a great impression on her contemporaries with her holiness and gentleness. It is said that Queen Adela, wife of King Louis VII, sought out her advice.

Feast Day: November 3

Saint Gerald of Aurillac
855–909

Born in Saint-Cirques in France, he was the count of Aurillac. A wealthy nobleman, he was known for his generosity and piety. He founded a Benedictine abbey on his Aurillac estate. He was blind during the latter years of his life.

He is also the Patron Saint of bachelors.

Feast Day: October 14

Saint Giles
Dates unknown

In the Middle Ages he was one of the most popular Saints. More than 150 churches throughout Europe have been dedicated to him. However, very little is known for certain about his life. It is said that he protected his pet hind or stag from a king's arrow by receiving the wound himself.

Feast Day: September 1

Saint Henry
973–1024

Born a duke in Bavaria in Germany, he ascended to the throne of Imperial Emperor in 1002 and was crowned Holy Roman Emperor in 1014 by Pope Benedict VIII. Being a sovereign, much of his life history is connected with the history of Europe and the church during his reign. Known as Henry the Good, he became lame in his later years.

Feast Day: July 13

Saint Seraphina
Died 1253

Born to poor parents in Tuscany, Italy, she suffered many diseases in her youth, one of which left her paralyzed on one side. However, it is said that she bore her suffering with a kind heart and cheerful spirit, never losing her faith in God. According to stories, after she died, the scent of flowers came from her grave.

Feast Day: March 12

Saint Servulus

  Died circa A.D. *590*

A cripple who begged for alms at Saint Clement's church in Rome, he was known for sharing what he received with other beggars. The neighborhood around Saint Clement's is said to have revered this beggar for he had memorized whole books of the Bible and sang hymns of praise despite his infliction. He is interred at Saint Clement's.

Feast Day: December 23

Saint Pantaleon (Panteleimon) of Nicomedia
Died A.D. 305

Born in what is now Turkey, he was the son of a Christian mother and pagan father. He was the personal doctor of Emperor Maximianus Herculeus, but is also said to have treated the poor without payment. Falsely accused by another doctor, he was sentenced to death, but each method employed failed. He was tied to a wheel, which broke; thrown to wild beasts, which did not attack him; and thrown into the water, but floated back to shore. In frustration, the executioners nailed his hands to his head and then finally beheaded him. It is said that after his head was severed, milk, not blood, flowed from his wounds.

The name Pantaleon, taken from the name Panteleemon, means "compassion for all people."

He is also the Patron Saint of doctors, midwives, livestock, helper of crying children, and invoked against locusts, loneliness, accidents, and consumption.

Feast Day: September 11

Saint Teresa of Avila
1515–1582

Sometimes called the "roving nun," she founded the first reformed convent of Saint Joseph in her native Spain. She was a tireless worker, opening many convents throughout her life. However, she was also plagued with headaches, partly attributed to malaria, throughout her life. She was also blessed with many mystical experiences and it is said that, following her death, the imprint of a cross was found on her heart.

She is also the Patron Saint against "Sorrows of the Heart."

Feast Day: October 15

Saint Peter Damiani
1007–1072

Mistreated as a child, he was given the lowliest tasks, such as pig herding, until joining an order of hermit monks. He devoted his life to writing and preaching against abuses of the Church at the time. Chief among these was the dependence of the Church on the government.

Feast Day: February 21

Saint John of God
1495–1550

Born in Portugal, he worked at various times as a soldier, shepherd, and peddler. After hearing a sermon by Saint John Avila, he felt overwhelming guilt and mended his ways. He eventually settled in Grenada, where he looked after the sick and dying. He helped to found the order of the Brothers Hospitallers.

Along with Saint Camillus de Lellis, he is also the Patron Saint of the sick, hospitals, and nurses. He is also the Patron Saint of booksellers.

Feast Day: March 8

Saint Drogo
Died 1189

He left his Flemish home to become a shepherd in France. He was renowned early for his many acts of grace, including self-mortification and his numerous pilgrimages to Rome. However, he ended his journeys to Rome when he became afflicted with a severe hernia. So ashamed of his affliction, Drogo became a hermit in a small room built for him in a church. It was in this room that he spent the remaining forty years of his life.

He is also the Patron Saint of those suffering from mental illness, as well as those who are ugly, and orphans.

Feast Day: April 16

Saint Blaise
Died A.D. 316

A bishop in Armenia, he was martyred under Licinius's persecutions. It is said that he once saved a young boy from choking to death after the youth swallowed a fish bone. He is also the Patron Saint of doctors, building employees, wind musicians, plasterers, pets, masons, tailors, cobblers, weavers, and invoked against diseases and ailments of the neck.

Feast Day: February 3

Saint Roch (Saint Rock)
Circa 1295–1327

Very little is known about this Saint, except that during the plague in Italy, he helped to nurse the sick and dying throughout that country. It is said that he himself contracted the plague, but recovered. He is also the Patron Saint of pestilence and skin diseases.

He is also the Patron Saint of bachelors.

Feast Day: August 17

Saint Antony of Egypt
251–356

The patriarch of all monks, he was the first to gather male followers together in communities. Born in Upper Egypt, at the age of twenty he gave away all his possessions to the poor and became a hermit. Fifteen years later, he went into the desert in a test of devotion. Later, he formed what was to become the first monastery.

Famed throughout Egypt and beyond, he was sought by both religious and secular rulers for his advice on a variety of matters. He is the Patron Saint of those afflicted with skin rashes because it is said that he most likely suffered with a contagious form of what we today call erysipelas— a bacterial infection that causes skin inflammation.

He is also the Patron Saint of the poor, the sick, and domestic animals.

Feast Day: January 17

Saint James the Greater
Died A.D. 44

All that is to be found of this Apostle is in the Gospels. He was a fisherman and brother of the Apostle John. He is also the Patron Saint of Spain, but why he is the Patron Saint of those suffering from rheumatism remains unclear.

He is also the Patron Saint of orphans.

Feast Day: July 25

Saint Ursula and companions
  Circa A.D. 900

In one of the most popular legends of the Middle Ages, it is said that Saint Ursula was raised the daughter of an English king. Rather than marry a pagan, she fled with a number of young women, all virgins. Although the original number of women following her began at ten, the number in stories grew to one thousand, then to ten thousand. The story follows their travels by ship, first from England and then to Germany, and finally to Rome, where the women were martyred when shot by the arrows of invading Huns.

She is also the Patron Saint of women teachers, cloth traders, and the Sorbonne University in Paris, France.

Feast Day: October 21

Saint Camillus de Lellis
1550–1614

A soldier and gambler, following his conversion, he tried to join the order of the Capuchins, but was denied because of a foot disease. Seeking to turn his life to a good cause, he became the director of a hospital and spent the remainder of his days caring for the sick. He also established many orders throughout Italy to care for the sick and dying.

He is also the Patron Saint of the sick and the dying and their nurses.

Feast Day: July 14

Saint Germaine of Pibrac (Germaine Cousin)
1579–1601

She was the daughter of a poor farmer in France. Born with a crippled right hand and general poor health, she was ignored by her father and her stepmother treated her cruelly. She tended sheep and was known for her religious devotion, her capable ways in her job, and for the great kindnesses she bestowed on those less fortunate than her and on children. Several miraculous occurrences are attributed to this Saint.

She is also the Patron Saint of the abandoned, the ugly, and victims of child abuse.

Feast Day: June 15

Saint Quirinus of Neuss (Saint Grein)

Told to guard captive Christians by Emperor Hadrian, he soon discovered that Pope Alexander I was among his charges. Several stories abound regarding his conversion, one of which has Hermes and Pope Alexander in the same cell, after Quirinus separated them. Another story depicts Pope Alexander I curing Quirinus's daughter. Following his conversion, he and his daughter were put to death, suffering martyrs' fates.

He is also the Patron Saint of horses and is invoked against headaches, gout, and rheumatism.

Feast Day: April 30

Saint Willibrord
658–739

Given by his parents to the Scottish monks at Ripon, near York, he eventually became a Benedictine. Shortly thereafter, he went to Ireland and was consecrated a priest. After his entry into the Frisian mission, he was made bishop. Throughout his life he was a tireless worker in the name of Jesus.

He is also the Patron Saint of childhood diseases and epilepsy.

Feast Day: November 7

Saint Remigius of Rheims
Died A.D. 533

It is said that his birth was predicted by a blind hermit monk and that when he was born, the monk's sight returned. Legend has it that as a young bishop, he was so gentle that birds did not fear him. He is most renowned for the baptism of Clovis, the king of the Franks.

He is also the Patron Saint invoked against fevers, snakes, religious complacency, despair, and temptation.

Feast Day: October 1

Saint Erasmus (Elmo or Telmo)
  Died A.D. *303*

Also the Patron Saint of sailors (hence, St. Elmo's fire), he was a bishop who was revered throughout Europe in the Middle Ages. Sentenced to death, he was disemboweled and tortured for his faith.

He is also the Patron Saint of childbirth, and invoked against cattle plagues.

Feast Day: June 2

Saint Apollonia of Alexandria
Died A.D. 249

The daughter of the king, she renounced worldly goods and preached in Alexandria. It is said that a divine spirit led her to a hermit who baptized her. However, her preaching soon angered a "sorcerer" who incited a mob against her. The mob captured Saint Apollonia, dragging her and other Christian women through the streets, eventually torturing them by knocking out their teeth, then throwing them into a fire.

Feast Day: February 7

Saint Veronica
First century A.D.

The name given to the woman who wiped Christ's brow when he stumbled under the weight of the cross on his way to Calvary. The familiar story is that his face appeared on the cloth she used. The story continued when Emperor Tiberius sent for Jesus to plead for healing and discovered that Pilate had already crucified Christ. However, upon gazing on the cloth with Jesus' face, he was immediately healed.

Veronica is the Patron Saint of washerwomen and advocate for a "good" death.

Feast Day: July 12

Words of Divine Wisdom

—⟡—

The saints had no hatred, no bitterness.
They forgave everything.
—SAINT JOHN VIANNEY

It is human to fall, but angelic to rise again.
—SAINT MARY EUPHRASIA PELLETIER

Heaven is filled with converted sinners of all kinds and
there is room for more.
—SAINT JOSEPH CAFASSO

To sin is human, but to persist in sin is devilish.
—SAINT CATHERINE OF SIENA

All riches come from iniquity, and unless one has lost,
another cannot gain. Hence the common opinion
seems to be very true, "the rich man is unjust, or the
heir to an unjust one." Opulence is always the result
of theft, if not committed by the actual possessor, then
by his predecessor.
—SAINT JEROME

An iron is fashioned by fire and on an anvil, so in the
fire of suffering and under the weight of trials our
souls receive the form which Our Lord desires them
to have.
—SAINT MADELEINE-SOPHIE BARAT

Hate the sin, love the sinner.
—SAINT AUGUSTINE

*The way to overcome the devil when he excites feelings
of hatred for those who injure us
is immediately to pray for their conversion.*
—SAINT JOHN VIANNEY

Anger is a kind of temporary madness.
—SAINT BASIL

*It is not possible for all things to be well, unless all
men were good, which I think will not be this good
many years.*
—SAINT THOMAS MORE

ᴄᴏ

*B*ATTERED WIVES

Saint Godeleva (Godelive)
1045–1070

From almost the beginning of Godeleva's wedded life, she was ill treated by both her Flemish nobleman husband, Bertulf of Ghistelles, and her mother-in-law for unknown reasons. She was regularly beaten and suffered other abuses. After several years of abuse, her husband had her strangled and drowned while he was away so that he could not be convicted of the crime. Outrage over the crime and reports of miracles caused her to be venerated as a ''martyr'' locally. Her body was enshrined years after her death in the church of Ghistelles by the bishop of Tournai.

She is also the Patron Saint of unhappy or difficult marriages.

Feast Day: July 6

Saint Nunilo and Saint Alodia
Died A.D. 851

Daughters of a Christian mother and non-Christian stepfather, both sisters suffered terrible abuse and brutality for their faith. They were beheaded in 851.

Saint Nunilo is also the Patron Saint of single women.

Saint Alodia is also the Patron Saint of single women and runaway or missing children.

Feast Day: October 22

Saint Margaret the Barefoot
Died 1395

Born in San Servino, Italy, she was married at the age of fifteen. Abused by her husband, she withstood her suffering for many years. She is said to have gone barefoot in sympathy for the poor, for whom she begged.

She is also the Patron Saint of young brides, unhappy marriages, and widows.

Feast Day: August 27

Saint Monica
332–387

Born to Christian parents in North Africa, she married a pagan man, Patricius. Although Patricius was known to have a violent temper and to verbally scorn Saint Monica for her faith, it is unclear whether he ever actually beat Saint Monica. She had three children, the eldest of whom was Saint Augustine of Hippo. It is believed that her unfailing faith eventually led to the conversion of both Patricius and Saint Augustine. She died shortly after Saint Augustine's baptism, en route to Africa from Rome in 387. Her relics are in Saint Augustine's church in Rome.

Feast Day: August 27

Saint Pharaildis (Varlde, Verylde, or Veerle)
Died circa 740

Forced to marry against her will, Saint Pharaildis kept a vow of virginity throughout her life. It is generally believed that this vow caused her husband to physically abuse her. She is venerated in her native Flanders and is the patron saint of Ghent.

She is also the Patron Saint of unhappy marriages and widows.

Feast Day: January 4

Saint Margaret of Cortona
1247–1297

The daughter of a poor farmer in Tuscany, Italy, she became the mistress of a nobleman. However, when he died suddenly, she accepted the Lord into her life. Forsaking all but the most basic possessions, she devoted herself to good works and acts of kindness. However, even after she founded a hospital, she was plagued by gossip. It was said that she carried on "intimate" relations with one or more of her spiritual advisors. Only later was she acknowledged as devoting her life in service to others, while her visions and religious communications were also accepted.

She is also the Patron Saint of single women, the homeless, and midwives.

Feast Day: February 22

Saint Marina
Dates unknown

Dressed as a boy, she entered the monastery with her father. However, after his death and still dressed as a male, she was accused of fathering a child on a local innkeeper's daughter. As punishment, she was banished from the order and reduced to begging. Five years later, she returned to the monastery, offering to care for the child in order to gain readmittance. Allowed to return to the order with the child, she became the young boy's devoted guardian. It was only after her death that it was discovered she was, in fact, a woman.

Feast Day: February 12

Saint Blandina
Died circa A.D. 180

A slave girl at the time of Marcus Aurelius, she is perhaps one of the best known of the martyrs of Lyons. She was falsely accused of the most horrendous crimes, yet maintained her faith in God. Even under torture, she would not speak anything but the truth. And it is said that when she was lowered into an arena with beasts, the animals would not touch her.

Feast Day: June 2

Saint Simon of Trent
Died 1474

A twelve-year-old boy, he was a native of northern Italy when he was kidnapped, tortured, and crucified. Those accused, now thought falsely, were tortured for their confessions. However, following the youth's burial, miracles were reported at his gravesite. He is also the Patron Saint for victims of torture.

Feast Day: March 24

Saint Adelaide
930-999

Adelaide of Burgundy was imprisoned after the death of her husband, Lothair II of Italy, by Berengarius when she refused to marry his son, Adalbert. Her eventual escape was accomplished with the help of a priest, who assisted her in digging an escape hole through her cell's wall. She was married then to Otto the Great and was crowned empress by Pope John XII. She is additionally the Patron Saint of parents with large families.

Saint Adelaide is also the Patron Saint of stepparents, widows, and young brides.

Feast Day: December 16

Saint Dismas
Dates unknown

The "Good Thief," he and his accomplice, Gestas, robbed the Holy Family on their way to Egypt. It was Dismas, who persuaded his partner in crime not to harm the Holy Family. The baby Jesus, it is said, foresaw their crucifixions on Calvary.

Feast Day: March 25

Saint Leonard
  Sixth century A.D.

Greatly revered during the Middle Ages throughout all of England, France, Germany, and other parts of Europe, today very little is actually known about Saint Leonard. However, many miracles and acts of intercession have been attributed to him. It is also said that he was a hermit as well as a founder of a monastery in France and a crusader. The most popular and widespread story of his life recounts his leaving home for the Crusades, during which he was captured, then miraculously set free. Hence, he became the Patron Saint of prisoners.

Saint Leonard is also the Patron Saint of farmers, miners, metal smiths, load carriers, locksmiths, fruit merchants, women in labor, horses, and cattle.

Feast Day: November 6

Words of Divine Wisdom

———— ✧ ————

There is no such thing as bad weather. All weather is good because it is God's.
—SAINT TERESA OF AVILA

If everyone would take only according to his needs and would leave the surplus to the needy, no one would be rich, no one poor, no one in misery.
—SAINT BASIL

For it is for him to fear death who is not willing to go to Christ.
—SAINT CYPRIAN

Be diligent in serving the poor. Love the poor. Honor them as you would Christ himself.
—SAINT LOUISE DE MARILLAC

No one is really happy merely because he has what he wants, but only if he wants things he ought to want.
—SAINT AUGUSTINE

Sorrow can be alleviated by good sleep, a bath, and a glass of wine.
—SAINT THOMAS ACQUINAS

Our Lord takes pleasure in doing the will of those who love him.
—SAINT JOHN VIENNEY

Let the world indulge its madness, for it cannot endure and passes like a shadow. It is growing old, and I think, is in its last decrepit stage. But we,

buried deep in the wounds of Christ,
why should we be dismayed?
—SAINT PETER CANISIUS

Be not anxious about what you have,
but about what you are.
—SAINT GREGORY

He lacks everything who thinks he lacks nothing.
—SAINT BERNARD

A vice in the heart is an idol on the altar.
—SAINT JEROME

A man who governs his passions is master of the world.
—SAINT DOMINIC

The better friends you are, the straighter you can talk,
but while you are only on nodding terms, be slow to scold.
—SAINT FRANCIS XAVIER

We must adapt society to the times,
not the times to society.
—SAINT IGNATIUS OF LOYOLA

SPECIAL NEEDS

───────────────── ୶ ─────────

*A*GAINST THEFT

Saints Gervase and Protasius of Milan
   Dates unknown

The relics of these two martyrs were not discovered until
A.D. 386 and very little is known of their lives. However,
the legend that surrounds their deaths identifies them as
twins persecuted for their faith. It is said that they refused
to make a sacrifice to a pagan idol and were killed by
beating and beheading.

They are also Patron Saints of the good and healthy
flow of blood and urine.

Feast Day: June 19

Saint Bernard of Clairvaux
1090–1153

Born into royalty, he entered the monastery at an early age and became a powerful force in the Church. His good works include establishing more than sixty monasteries, preaching crusades throughout Europe, and counseling Popes. During his lifetime he received many divine visions and was tempted many times by Satan to no avail.

He is also Patron Saint invoked to ward off storms as well as to aid climbers in trouble.

Feast Day: August 20

Saint Adrian of Nicomedia
Died circa A.D. 304

A pagan officer in the imperial court of Nicomedia, he was arrested and imprisoned when he showed compassion and identified with the persecuted Christians. His loyal wife, Natalia, provided comfort for him and his fellow Christians after his arrest. Following his execution, she fled to Greece with his relics.

He is also the Patron Saint of soldiers, prison guards, and executioners.

Feast Day: September 8

Saint Catherine of Siena
1347–1380

Perhaps one of the greatest women in Christianity, she was born of humble parents and, when still a teenager, entered the order of Saint Dominic, though she remained at home. Her goodness and divine spirit brought many believers to her side. Most of her life was spent caring for those sick with the plague and the impoverished. However, she was also instrumental in persuading Pope Gregory XI to leave France for Rome. It is said that Christ gave her the divine wisdom to preach his word and that, in a divine vision, she "exchanged" hearts with Jesus.

She is also invoked against headaches and plague.

Feast Day: April 29

Saint Birgitta (Bridget) of Sweden
  1304–1391

Happily married for twenty-eight years and the mother of
eight children, she performed her duties with cheerfulness
and charity to the poor. She became a lady-in-waiting to
the queen of Sweden. After her husband died, she settled
in a monastery and beheld many divinely inspired revelations and founded an order called the Bridgettines. A book
of her revelations has been translated into numerous lan-
guages and is still read today.

Feast Day: July 23

Saint John the Apostle
  First century A.D.

The disciple whom Jesus loved and to whom he entrusted the care of his mother. He was a fisherman and younger brother of Saint James the Greater. The author of the gospel which bears his name, he was the only one of the Twelve Apostles who was not a martyr. Many legends and miracles are attributed to him.

St. John is also the Patron Saint of miners, sculptors, bookbinders, printers, booksellers, engravers, portrait painters, basket makers, notaries, paper manufacturers, authors, mirror makers, and is invoked against epilepsy, bad feet, poisoning, burns, and hailstorms.

Feast Day: December 27

The Seven Sleepers of Ephesus

According to legend, the seven youths hid in a cave to avoid making pagan sacrifices. When the Emperor Decius discovered their plot, he had the cave sealed up with them in it. It is said that when the cave was unsealed more than three hundred years later, the seven youths awoke.

They are also considered Patron Saints of sailors and are invoked against fever.

Feast Day: July 27

Saint Anthony (Antony) of Padua
1195–1231

Often known as the "Wonder Worker" for his powers of intercession, Saint Anthony of Padua is also the Patron Saint of travelers. He was born in Portugal, and he preached in both Italy and France. It is said that he spoke so powerfully that men closed their places of business to hear him speak. He was called the "hammer of the heretics."

However, Saint Anthony is most famous as a retriever of lost items. Literally tens of thousands have attributed his intercession to reuniting them with their belongings. And, in Saint's Mass, the verse reads, "The Lord shall place him over all his goods."

He is also the Patron Saint of lovers, married couples, women, children, horses, and donkeys. He is also invoked against infertility, fever, shipwreck, war, and plague.

Feast Day: June 13

Saint Afra of Augsburg
Died circa A.D. 300

Very little is known for certain of Saint Afra. A converted Christian, she was martyred under Diocletian's rule. Among the many legends which surround her, most prominent is the one that she owned a house of ill repute. It is said that during the persecutions, Bishop Narcissus of Gerona found her house and mistakenly took it for an inn. Afra, then a pagan, was converted upon hearing the bishop pray. It is also said that she saved Narcissus from certain death by hiding him.

She is also the Patron Saint of penitents and lost souls.

Feast Day: August 5

Saint Helen (Helena)
248–330

The mother of Constantine the Great, she was widely known for her generosity to the poor and the building of many churches throughout the Middle East. The legend surrounding her life has Saint Helen discovering the "true" cross of Christ in a well in Jerusalem.

She is also the Patron Saint of miners and treasure hunters.

Feast Day: August 18

Saint Vincent de Paul
1580–1660

He entered the priesthood at the age of twenty, a callow young man who enjoyed worldly pleasures. However, during a journey to Paris, he saw firsthand the poverty around him. From then on he dedicated his life to helping the poor and less fortunate. This involved not only establishing charitable orders, including the one that bears his name, but helping to organize soup kitchens and other institutions that saved many lives in his lifetime and after.

In addition to being the Patron Saint of lost objects, he is also the Patron Saint of charitable institutions, prisoners, hospitals, and orphanages.

Feast Day: September 27

Saint Notburga of Rattenberg
1265–1313

Born of humble parents in Bavaria, she was employed as a servant to a noble family. She was dismissed for giving food to the poor, but later reinstated in the position of servant. Known for her devotion, it is said that a pair of oxen returned her body to the town of Eben.

She is also the Patron Saint of maids, and invoked for a good birth and against sickness in cattle.

Feast Day: September 14

Saint Barnabas
First century A.D.

Although not ''officially'' an Apostle, he is often viewed as one in the wider sense. His real name was Joseph the Levite, but the Apostles gave him the name Barnabas, which means ''the son of consolation.'' Among his good acts mentioned, is the way he sold his land and placed the money at the feet of the Apostles; introduced Saul to the Apostles; and preached with Paul in Antioch.

He is also the Patron Saint invoked against quarrels and hailstorms.

Feast Day: June 11

Saint Juliana of Cumae
Died A.D. 305

Not much is known of this Saint, who was martyred near Naples. Legend says that she was killed under the rule of Diocletian when she wouldn't marry a pagan. While she was awaiting execution, the devil appeared to her in the form of an angel and tried to talk her into the marriage. Instead of surrendering to his arguments, which surely would have saved her life, she literally fought the devil off with the chains that held her. When it came time for her execution, angels destroyed the instruments of her death until her tormentors were forced to behead her.

Feast Day: February 16

AGAINST FIRE

Saint Thecla
Dates unknown

A follower of Paul the Apostle, she renounced her past ways and abandoned her bridegroom after her conversion. Condemned to be burned at the stake, she was miraculously saved by a hail- and thunderstorm. Later, she was sentenced to be devoured by wild beasts, but the animals did not touch her. Once released from prison, she converted both her own mother and her abandoned bridegroom.

She is also the Patron Saint against plague and invoked for the dying.

Feast Day: September 23

Saint Scholastica
480–543

The sister of Saint Benedict, she was a devout virgin who lived in the Benedictine nunnery of Roccabotte. It is said that she met with her brother once a year to engage in spiritual discussions. However, on their last meeting, her prayers and tears started a storm that forced him to extend his visit. It is also said that after her death, Saint Benedict reported seeing her soul rise to heaven in the form of a white dove.

Feast Day: February 10

Saint Januarius of Benevento
(Janiver, Gennaro, Jenaro)
  Dates unknown

Very little is known of this Saint and martyr, except that
he was beheaded in Italy near Pozzuoli, under the cruel
reign of Diocletian. He was sentenced to death after refusing to make a pagan sacrifice. It is said that when wild
beasts were unleashed to kill him they settled passively at
his feet. He was killed along with his companions, Acut-
ius, Desiderius, Eutyches, Proculus, and the deacons Fes-
tus and Sosius.

Feast Day: September 19

Saint Helen (Helena)
248-330

The mother of Constantine the Great, she was widely known for her generosity to the poor and the building of many churches throughout the Middle East. The legend surrounding her life has Helen discovering the "true" cross of Christ in a well in Jerusalem.

She is also the Patron Saint of miners and treasure hunters.

Feast Day: August 18

Saint Columbanus (Kolumban or Columban)
543–615

He founded the great monastery of Luxeuil with twelve
followers. It is said that his rules were very strict and
strictly imposed. When he challenged the king on grounds
of the ruler's immorality, he was banished to Burgundy,
where he lived for two years, before moving to Italy,
where he founded another monastery.

He is also the Patron Saint of Ireland and invoked
against mental illness.

Feast Day: November 23

Saint Ulrich (Ulric) of Augsburg
890–973

He began his religious training early and rose through the
religious ranks. As a bishop in what is now Germany, he
had a strong wall built around the city that foiled repeated
raids by Hungarians. He later helped lead an army against
the invading Hungarians. It is said that he miraculously
rode through a raging river.

In addition to being the Patron Saint against floods, he
is also the Patron Saint of all those in danger from water.

Feast Day: July 4

Saint Bernard of Clairvaux
1090–1153

Born into royalty, he entered the monastery at an early age and became a powerful force in the Church. His good works included establishing more than sixty monasteries, preaching crusades throughout Europe, and counseling Popes. During his lifetime he received many divine visions and was tempted many times by Satan to no avail.

He is also the Patron Saint invoked at the hour of death as well as by climbers in trouble.

Feast Day: August 20

Saint Clement (Clemens or Klemens)
Died A.D. 101

The third Pope, after Saint Peter, he governed for ten years. It is said that he was thrown into the ocean by the Emperor Trajan with an anchor around his neck and his body was found on the sea floor in a chapel built by angels.

He is also the Patron Saint of children and stonemasons, and is invoked against disaster at sea.

Feast Day: November 23

Saint Paul the Apostle
Died circa A.D. 65

Well educated, he worked as a tentmaker before his conversion, but his life was changed after his conversion. As a missionary, he made three journeys to spread the word of God. However, on his third journey he was arrested and jailed. Martyred in Rome, it is said that three springs grew from the site where his head fell to the earth.

Saint Paul is also the Patron Saint of laborers, theologians, weavers, basket makers, rope makers, and is invoked against snakebites and for rain.

Feast Day: June 29

Words of Divine Wisdom

It is little use expecting anything from the mighty ones of this world—for the most part they leave the poor to their poverty, and mean and ungenerous as they are, turn a deaf eye to the cry of those who are weak and helpless.
—SAINT PLACID RICCARDI

If you would rise, shun luxury, for luxury lowers and degrades.
—SAINT JOHN CHRYSOSTOM

You who have the kingdom of heaven, are not a poor little woman, but a queen.
—SAINT JORDAN OF SAXONY

When you wish to give alms but your thought brings doubt as to whether it is best not to give, test your thought and if you find that the doubt comes from avarice, give a little more than you intended.
—SAINT BARSANUPHIUS

*Be diligent in serving the poor.
Honor them, as you would Christ himself.*
—SAINT LOUISE DE MARILLAC

A man's poverty before God is judged by the disposition of his heart, not by his coffers.
—SAINT AUGUSTINE OF HIPPO

*Riches are the instrument of all vices,
because they render us capable of putting
even our worst desires into execution.*
—SAINT AMBROSE

He is rich enough who is poor with Christ.
—SAINT JEROME

The poor monk is lord of the world.
—SAINT JOHN CLIMACUS

*Renunciation of riches is the origin
and preserver of virtues.*
—SAINT AMBROSE

*When you experience humiliation, you should take it as
a sure sign that some grace is in store.*
—SAINT BERNARD

*The more we despise poverty the more will the world
despise us and the greater need will we suffer. But
if we embrace Holy Poverty very closely, the world will
come to us and will feed us abundantly.*
—SAINT FRANCIS OF ASSISI

———— ∾ ————

Saint Armogastes
  Died A.D. *455*

This martyr held a prominent position in the court of King Genseric. When the king renounced his faith and began persecuting Christians, Saint Armogastes was horribly tortured before banishment. However, he viewed suffering for his belief in Christ as contributing to God's greater glory.

Feast Day: March 29

Saint Antony of Egypt
  Born A.D. *251*

Duly called the "patriarch of all monks," it is said that he gave away all his possessions to the poor at the age of twenty. He then became a hermit, living a simple life that attracted the attention of rulers as well as commoners. His wisdom was much prized and his miracles became famous throughout the Middle East. It is said that he resisted all temptations, both those plotted by Satan and the more mundane sort posed by men.

  He is also Patron Saint of the sick, butchers, and domestic animals.

Feast Day: January 17

Saint John the Almsgiver of Alexandria
  Sixth century A.D.

Following the death of his children and wife, he began life again as an ascetic. It is said that he sold his own sheets to give alms to the poor; that he adopted a boy whose father could no longer afford to feed him; that he supported another impoverished merchant; and that he gave alms to all who asked. When he was elected Patriarch of Alexandria, he fought tirelessly against heretics.

  He is also Patron Saint of ship workers, charity, and merchants of all kinds.

Feast Day: January 23

Saint Julia

  Sixth or seventh century A.D.

A young peasant girl from Corsica, she was sold as a slave to a pagan merchant from Syria. Although sentenced to a life of menial labor, she performed her duties with the divine knowledge that her life was one chosen by God.

Feast Day: May 22

Saint Saturus

  Died A.D. 455

Like Armogastes, Saturus suffered in Africa under the Vandal King Genseric. A wealthy landowner, he was threatened by the king and officials with the loss of all possessions should he not renounce his faith. Though his family begged him to renounce his faith, he held strong and thus lost all worldly possessions he once cherished. Like Armogastes, he was horribly tortured, condemned to menial tasks, and died in poverty.

Feast Day: March 29

Words of Divine Wisdom

———— ❧ ————

*Every creature in the world will raise up hearts to God
if we look upon it with a good eye.*
—SAINT FELIX OF CANALICE

*We admire the Creator, not only as the framer of
heaven and earth, of sun and ocean ... [as well as]
bears and lions, but also as the maker of tiny creatures:
ants, gnats, flies ...*
—SAINT JEROME

*Every time I do not behave like a donkey, it is the
worse for me. How does a donkey behave? If it is
slandered, it keeps silent; if it is not fed, it keeps
silent; if it is forgotten, it keeps silent; it never
complains, however much it is beaten or ill used,
because it has a donkey's patience. That is how
the servant of God must behave. I stand before you,
Lord, like a donkey.*
—SAINT PETER CLAVER

*Every creature is by its nature a kind of effigy and
likeness of the eternal Wisdom ...*
—SAINT BONAVENTURE

*Never did Saint Dominic, even on his journeys, eat meat
or any dish cooked with meat ...*
—SAINT JORDAN OF SAXONY

*Be ye prudent as the serpent who, in danger, exposes
his whole body to preserve his head. In the same*

way, we must risk everything, if necessary, to preserve the love and presence of Our Lord . . .
—SAINT FRANCIS DE SALES

Speak little to creatures, but speak much with God.
—SAINT MARY MAZZARELLO

CATTLE

Saint Oswald
604–642

The king of Northumbria, he has in the past been honored as one of the great heroes of England. It is said that upon his coronation as king, a raven miraculously delivered the needed oil for the ceremony. Another raven, it is said, delivered a gold ring with which he was to be betrothed to the daughter of another king.

He is also the Patron Saint of crusaders, weather, reapers, and those in need.

Feast Day: August 5

Saint Gall
550–645

He was one of the twelve monks who left Ireland with Saint Columban. He later became a missionary hermit in a variety of places, most significantly on the spot where Saint Gall now stands in Switzerland.

It is said that Saint Gall and Saint Columban performed a variety of miracles associated with converting pagans to Christianity. However, one of the most enduring stories involves the building of a chapel in which a beam miraculously "grew" to fit into its place in the structure.

He is also the Patron Saint of fever patients.

Feast Day: October 16

161

Saint Stephen of Hungary (Stephen I)
970–1038

The son of Hungary's ruler, Arpád, he unified the country and people into a Christian state, successfully fighting off all pagan reactions to his social change. He was by all accounts considered a good and just king. Many legends surround his life, including miraculous cures of the sick.

Feast Day: August 16

Saint Maurice of Agaunum
Died circa A.D. 287

One of the martyrs of the Theban Legion comprised of Christian soldiers serving the Roman Emperor. While in Gaul, the men of the legion refused to make a pagan sacrifice or kill innocent Christians. Maximilan, (later Roman Emperor) then ordered every tenth soldier killed. When the men persisted in not carrying out the orders of pagan sacrifice, again every tenth man was killed, until the entire legion was wiped out.

Saint Maurice is also the Patron Saint of crusaders, dyers, clothiers, glass painters, hatters, soldiers, infantrymen, vineyards, clothing manufacturers, merchants, and armorers.

Feast Day: September 22

Saint Patrick
Fifth century A.D.

The Patron Saint and Apostle of Ireland, the story of his life is well-known. At the age of sixteen he was carried off as a slave to Ireland. He escaped after six years and was eventually consecrated a bishop. He traveled far and wide throughout Ireland, converting people to Christianity by teaching, example, and the miracles he performed.

He is also the Patron Saint of lost souls, miners, coopers, blacksmiths, and hairdressers.

Feast Day: March 17

Saint Cornelius

Died A.D. 253

The first Pope to confront the first formal Antipope. The first to suffer the persecution under Gallus. When ordered to make a sacrifice to a pagan god, he refused, but even after torture, still performed a miracle in healing a Roman soldier's wife.

He is also the Patron Saint of those with nervous disorders and against epilepsy.

Feast Day: September 16

Saint Walburga
710–779

The daughter of the King of England, and sister of Saint Willibald and Saint Winebald of Eichstatt, she was educated at a convent and when Saint Boniface began his missionary work with the Germans, she was sent along with other nuns to accompany him. She eventually became the abbess of a double monastery in Germany founded by her brother.

Many legends surround Saint Walburga. It is said that when Satan caused a storm at sea, her prayers quieted the waters. She is also credited with the miraculous healing of the lord of a castle in Germany. Further, to this day, believers in her power attribute miraculous healing power to the "oil" that gathers at the rock near her shrine in Heidenheim, Germany.

She is also the Patron Saint of prospering orchards, and invoked against dog bites, and rabies.

Feast Day: February 25

Saint George of Cappadocia
Died circa A.D. 305

Certainly one of the most popular Saints as well as the Patron Saint of soldiers. It is said that he was a high-ranking officer in the Roman army. Serving Rome in the Middle East, near what is today called Libya, legend has it that he killed a dragon that was terrorizing the town. After his conversion to Christianity, he was thrown into prison by the Emperor Diocletian, where Christ visited him in a vision. Various stories outline the tortures Saint George underwent at the hands of Diocletian's minions and how Saint George caused the pagan temple to collapse by praying.

He is also the Patron Saint of peasants and is invoked against plague, leprosy, syphilis, and snakebite.

Feast Day: April 23

Words of Divine Wisdom

---◇◆◇---

*In building we need not act as the people of the world
do. They first procure the money and then begin to
build, but we must do just the opposite. We will begin
to build and then expect to receive what is necessary
from Divine Providence.*
—SAINT ALPHONSUS LIGUORI

*The church of the Lord is built upon the rock of the
apostle among countless dangers in the world; it
therefore remains unmoved. The Church's foundation
is unshakable and firm against the assaults of the
raging sea ... Although the elements of this world con-
stantly batter and crash against her, she offers the
safest harbor of salvation for all in distress.*
—SAINT AMBROSE

*Do not be anxious about a house on earth when we
have such a beautiful one in Heaven.*
—SAINT SOLEDAD

HOSPITALS

Saint Getrude of Nivelles
626–659

The daughter of King Pépin the Elder, she entered the monastery founded by her mother in Nivelles after her father died. As the monastery's abbess, she instituted many reforms and performed her duties with selfless energy. During her lifetime, she founded a hospital and assisted in spreading the word of God by bringing more and more books from Rome. It is said that she assists the dead on their first night in heaven and that during her lifetime she performed many miracles, including reviving a drowned child and saving a knight who gave his soul over to the devil.

She is also the Patron Saint of travelers, pilgrims, and a helper during plagues.

Feast Day: March 17

Saint Charles Borromeo
1538–1584

A nobleman by birth, he entered the religious life early, then went on to study law. As a cardinal and as an archbishop, he devoted his life to Christ and the spreading of the gospel. He founded several seminaries, one specifically for missionaries. Among his written works was a manual for the instruction of children, more than two hundred years before the first instruction of youth was officially established. It is said that he saw a vision of an angel sliding a sword back into a scabbard that foretold the end of the plague. Throughout his life Saint Charles worked tirelessly, combating ignorance and superstition while creating a new discipline within the clergy.

He is also the Patron Saint of seminaries and boarding schools.

Feast Day: November 4

Saint Gregory the Great
Died A.D. 604

The first monk to become Pope, Saint Gregory is credited
with many written works which continue to influence the
Church to this day. The son of a royal father and Saint
Sylvia, he sent Saint Augustine to England to convert the
British. It is said that he fed the poor and hungry when
he himself had little, and when a beggar came to his door
he gave him a silver bowl that was part of his mother's
inheritance. It is also related that when he was writing,
the Holy Ghost, in the form of a dove, came and sat on
his shoulder, inspiring him.

He is also the Patron Saint of scholars, wise men, teachers, musicians, and choir schools.

Feast Day: March 12

Definitions of Saints' Names

Agatha—the good
Agnes—pure one
Albert—noble or brilliant
Ambrose—divine
Andrew—strong/masculine
Angela—angel
Ann (Hannah)—grace
Anthony—inestimable
Barbara—the stranger
Basil—kingly
Benedict—blessed
Bernadette—brave like a bear
Catherine—pure
Cecelia—blind one
Charles—strong/masculine
Christopher—Christ bearer
Claudia—lame one
David—beloved
Dominic—belonging to God
Dorothy—gift of God
Elizabeth—consecrated to God
Emily—industrious
Francis—free
Henry—ruler
Hubert—bright of mind

Isabel—consecrated to God
Jerome—sacred name
Joan—God is gracious
John—God is gracious
Julia—youthful
Justin—just or fair
Katherine—pure
Kevin—gentle
Lucy—one who brings light
Luke—one who brings light
Mark—warlike
Martin—warlike
Matthew—gift of God
Michael—victorious people
Patrick—noble one
Paul—little
Peter—rock
Philip—lover of horses
Richard—powerful ruler
Rita—pearl
Robert—famous
Stephen—crowned one
Timothy—to honor God
Veronica—true image

A Glossary of Some Saints' Emblems

Following is a partial listing of the most popular artistic/ symbolic motifs used in portraying the Saints in paintings, stained glass, book illustrations, and statues.

Holding or Carrying a Church

In art this symbol is typically used to denote the founding of a church or monastery.

Saint Amandus
Saint Chad
Saint Petroc
Saint Winaloe
Saint Withurga

A Palm or a Sword

The Palm or the Sword are two of the most established and common symbols associated with martyred Saints. Following is a partial listing of some of the most well known of those Saints.

Saint Agnes
Saint Barbara
Saint Cyprian
Saint Dionysius
Saint Justina
Saint Lucy

Saint Matthew
Saint Mathias
Saint Michael
Saint Paul
Saint Peter
Saint Thomas à Becket

Pen or Book

This symbol denoted the Saint as one of exceptional mental and writing talents. In most cases it is used to denote Saints who were Doctors of the Church.

Saint Anne—holding a book
Saint Anthony—a book with the Holy Infant Jesus on it
Saint Boniface—a book run through with a sword or an axe
Saint Elizabeth of Hungary—a book with crowns lying on it
Saint Paul—a book with a sword lying on it
Saint Stephen—a book with stones lying on it
Saint Walburga—a book with a container of oil lying on it

Holding or Carrying Food

Saint Dorothy
Saint Elizabeth
Saint Frances of Rome
Saint Jane of Valois
Saint Margaret of Scotland
Saint Olav
Saint Romanus
Saint Rosalia

Holding the Holy Infant

Saint Anthony of Padua
Saint Christopher
Saint Elizabeth
Saint Mary the Blessed Virgin
Saint Rose
Saint Vincent De Paul

Clothed in a Suit of Armor

Saint Eligius
Saint George
Saint Joan of Arc
Saint Longinus
Saint Martin
Saint Michael
Saint Nabor

Saint Olav
Saint Quentin
Saint Quirinus
Saint Sebastian
Saint Secundus
Saint Theodore of Tyro

One or More Roses

Saint Cecelia
Saint Dorothy
Saint Elizabeth

Saint Rose
Saint Teres of Lisieux

A Selection of Some of the More Unusual Emblems

Carrying Intestines—Saint Vincent
Intestines hanging out from body—Saint Claudius
Intestines drawn out of the body—Saint Erasmus
Carrying breasts held on a plate—Saint Agatha
A bearded Virgin—Saint Wilgefortis
Three golden balls or three ingots, a symbol which persists
to this day as denoting a pawnbroker—Saint Nicholas of
Myra

Amazing and Inspiring True Stories of Divine Intervention

ANGELS
  by Hope Price   72331-X/$4.99 US

ANGELS AMONG US
  by Don Fearheiley   77377-5/$5.50 US/$7.50 Can

THE COMPLETE ANGEL
  by James N. Pruitt   78045-3/$5.50 US/$6.50 Can

MIRACLES   77652-9/$4.99 US/$5.99 Can
  by Don Fearheiley

BEYOND THE LIGHT
  by P.M.H. Atwater   72540-1/$5.50 US/$7.50 Can

FASCINATING BOOKS
OF SPIRITUALITY
AND PSYCHIC DIVINATION

CLOUD NINE: A DREAMER'S DICTIONARY
by Sandra A. Thomson
77384-8/$6.99 US/$7.99 Can

SECRETS OF SHAMANISM:
TAPPING THE SPIRIT POWER
WITHIN YOU
by Jose Stevens, Ph.D. and Lena S. Stevens
75607-2/$5.99 US/$6.99 Can

TAROT IN TEN MINUTES
by R.T. Kaser
76689-2/$12.00 US/$16.00 Can

THE LOVERS' TAROT
*by Robert Mueller, Ph.D., and Signe E. Echols, M.S.,
with Sandra A. Thomson*
76886-0/$11.00 US/$13.00 Can

SEXUAL ASTROLOGY
by Marlene Masini Rathgeb
76888-7/$11.00 US/$15.00 Can

AMERICA'S MOST INSPIRATIONAL AUTHOR

BEYOND OUR SELVES
72202-X / $8.00 US/ $10.00 Can

TO LIVE AGAIN
72236-4/ $8.00 US/ $10.00 Can

A MAN CALLED PETER
72204-6/ $9.00 US/ $12.00 Can

SOMETHING MORE
72203-8/ $9.00 US/ $12.00 Can

THE HELPER
72282-8/ $8.00 US/ $10.00 Can

CATHERINE MARSHALL'S STORY BIBLE
69961-3/ $10.95 US/ $13.95 Can

THE BEST OF CATHERINE MARSHALL
72383-2/ $9.00 US/ $12.00 Can

Are you feeling OK about yourself?
Or still playing destructive games?

THE 15-MILLION-COPY
NATIONAL BESTSELLER BY
Thomas A. Harris, M.D.

I'M OK—
YOU'RE OK

00772-X/ $5.99 US/ $7.99 Can

**The Transactional Analysis Breakthrough that's
Changing the Consciousness and Behavior of People
Who Never Felt OK about Themselves.**

In *I'M OK—YOU'RE OK* find the freedom to change,
to liberate your adult effectiveness and to achieve a
joyful intimacy with the people in your life!

*And continue with a practical program for lifelong
well-being with*

STAYING OK

70130-8/$4.95 US/$5.95 Can

by Amy Bjork Harris
and Thomas A. Harris, M.D.

on how to maximize good feelings, minimize bad ones,
and live life to the fullest!

BARRY LOPEZ

DESERT NOTES: Reflections in the Eye of a Raven and
RIVER NOTES: The Dance of Herons
71110-9/ $9.00 US/ $12.00 Can

"Barry Lopez is a landscape artist who paints images with sparse, elegant strokes...His prose is as smooth as river rocks."

Oregon Journal

GIVING BIRTH TO THUNDER, 71111-7
SLEEPING WITH HIS DAUGHTER $9.00 US/ $12.00 Can

In 68 tales from 42 American Indian tribes, Lopez recreates the timeless adventures and rueful wisdom of Old Man Coyote, an American Indian hero with a thousand faces—and a thousand tricks.

WINTER COUNT 71937-1/ $7.00 US/ $9.00 Can

Quiet, intoxicating tales of revelation and woe evoke beauty from darkness, magic without manipulation, and memory without remorse.

FIELD NOTES: 72482-0
The Grace Note of the Canyon Wren $9.00 US/ $12.00 Can